July 2024

FEAR Is A Liar

Believing the Truth, Not the Lie

FEAR Is A Liar

Believing the Truth, Not the Lie

Finding Your Purpose

ANDY DIETZ

ABooks PUBLISHING

Printed in the United States of America

First Printing, 2018
ISBN-10: 1719495653
ISBN-13: 9781719495653

ABooksPublishing@gmail.com
www.andydietz.net

In honor of

My wife and best friend, Becky

for her passion to know Christ

and to seek the Truth with all her heart.

To my eleven grandchildren

and their generation,

that they may know the truth

and the truth will set them free.

Table of Contents

forward

Truth no longer seems important in our society today. Apologetics and the reasonable exchange of ideas have been destroyed by a radical movement of hate and intolerance, designed to shout down and malign anyone of an opposite, and especially conservative view. Little or no debate results in ideas and beliefs that may or may not be correct short of the reasoning process.

I doubt anyone would want to buy a new vehicle without driving it first. One should, at least, compare prices with another dealer to be sure you're getting the best product for the price. We have all bought that pair of jeans without trying them on, only to find that they didn't fit properly.

Shouldn't we all have a desire to test truth, to be sure that the position we are supporting is correct? The obvious answer should be "yes," but today it seems that truth doesn't matter.

Fear is a Liar, explores the "movement" to devalue truth, as a path to impose a "new faith' in our world, and to "fundamentally change America."

John J. Dunphy, Humanist magazine 1983: "Humanism is a religion with mankind as its god." He said, "Which will replace the rotting corpse of Christianity."

Truth is important! Truth helped lead to the discovery of America. The truth when used as a basis of one's guilt or innocence is important. Truth in relationships can result in stronger trust. We need truth, and without it, our society will fail!

We will also explore and focus on personal truth and the principles to discover your purpose in life. Truth, as a resolution to fear, anger, depression, and many other strongholds, which we all experience, is accessible to anyone desiring to learn that truth. I'll share the answers which brought healing to me, and to many others.

Truth is a vital part of our lives and without it, we resort to intolerance with one another and conclusions which may produce tragic consequences.

If truth does not exist, then the argument on its behalf is pointless. If truth does exist, then those who ignore it are foolish for their ignorance of it!

It is hard to imagine that anyone would be opposed to truth and the pursuit of It unless it exposes the perceived prosperity of their lie.

As a dyslexic, I never thought I would write, but I know these principles of truth and purpose are too important to allow my fear of writing to win!

Examine the presentation of truth in this book and if you haven't gained from it, the loss may only be two or three hours of read-time and a few bucks. However, the result might be priceless! Fear is a liar!

Introduction

Have you ever asked yourself, "Where is the life?" "What is the point to anything I am doing?" "Am I making a difference?" "What is my purpose in life?"

If we will be honest, I think most of us have asked some of the same questions. When we are alone in our own thoughts, and it is quiet with no distractions there to interrupt, I think we've all had similar questions and thoughts. Everyone wants to know if they are fulfilling their purpose and what that purpose might actually be. Does God really have a purpose for us, and is He desiring to show us that purpose, or is it even true?

A genuine debate about truth is underway in our world from both the religious person to the admitted atheist. Many have been in the church all their lives and yet others have never even considered God or religion at all. The truth debate may originate from those disappointed with organized religion, or perhaps from the question everyone has always asked anyway, "Is there a God?"

Regardless of the source, I believe there is a natural desire in every human to find the answer. I believe we are all created for a purpose, and that everyone has an internal need to know that purpose whether we believe in God or not.

I have discovered that those who really want to know the answer to this question will allow any reasonable solution to be examined. Those who have already concluded that there is no God, or no "real truth," will often shut themselves off to anything or anyone who may challenge their viewpoint, even with facts!

The essential question: "does it really matter?" Does it matter whether there is or isn't a God? Not to oversimplify the answer, but it does matter! It does matter if God actually exists but, if there is no existence of a true God then, it doesn't matter. This reasoning would be similar to knowing whether or not gravity exists while standing on the edge of the Royal Gorge bridge, ready to jump, without a parachute. At that point gravity, or the lack thereof *does* matter! Truth matters!

INTRODUCTION

I believe genuine truth brings joy and contentment; anything else will only bring isolation, loneliness, and continued searching for that truth!

Truth is defined as "a standard or authenticity" which, when absent, leaves one asking questions about oneself that seldom results in satisfactory answers. Questions, absent of truth, will naturally lead to conclusions lacking little completion or contentment.

When facing personal struggles, one needs truth to be exposed to those struggles to discover the resolution inside. We can apply the need for truth to physical, mental, spiritual, and even political situations. The problem, in the last decade, has been that the standard by which we measure truth seems to change. The standard never actually changes for truth, but society wants to change the "standard" to meet their personal qualifications and agendas.

I believe so many questions are being asked because the lines keep moving and the standard, or truth is being distorted. The real question should be, what is the truth? Truth is screaming to be discovered within us and around us. It is, however, the answer and the result, that doubters seem to reject.

My first understanding and discovery of truth began in my high school and college years. I probably knew a need for truth at a younger age, but I remember the light bulb coming on much later.

I'm not one to get depressed, but sometimes discouragement will creep in if I allow it. The nearest I came to depression was during my college days when the pressure of finances, new relationships, grades, tests, and the fact that this whole "college thing" became my responsibility. At times, that did make me want to quit, especially the day a guy took a leap off the fifth-floor balcony of my dorm, just as afternoon classes released. I never did get depressed enough to want to end it like that, but things did occasionally get very overwhelming for me.

My parents couldn't do it for me anymore, they were in another city, and my friends, for the most part, weren't around to cheer me on…it was all me. I was now the individual responsible to graduate and choose a career. College was unlike high school where everyone knew me, and the teachers wanted to see me succeed. In college, everyone had been the class "something" and the "Mister it." I could no longer make it on my accomplishments and celebrity because no one was really concerned, they had their own difficulties. There were, however, some professors and friends I met during the process who did help a little when they could, but I actually had to work hard, and step up and do it, because no one was going to do it for me. This was my "Rite of Passage!"

That was college, and graduation was the biggest relief of my life! Since that time, I have discovered that life is still full of challenges and many of the questions remain.

When the questions and challenges come, we could quit, many people do, or we could search for the answers and solutions.

Since college, I have had many successes, and I have been blessed in so many ways. I have a wonderful soul mate in my wife Becky, four fantastic kids, and eleven awesome grandchildren. Still, with all that, questions sometimes remain. It was fifteen years ago that I finally sought the answers, earnestly, with all my heart. I knew there had to be an answer to LIFE! I knew Christ as Savior, which was never in question, but I think I wanted to make better sense of the "life" He had given me to live.

I found myself "living" this thing called life, but where was the actual LIFE? I must admit that all was going fairly well for me after college. I didn't experience anything near the discouragement that I felt as a student. Still, I realized I was searching for something; I didn't know what it was for sure but knew I needed to find out.

Being in the ministry, I counsel many people who struggle with the same questions that I've had, and even deeper ones. I wanted to help, and give them solutions as well, so I knew there had to be an answer.

When God began to reveal His truth to my wife and me through what we call the "truth principle," we were over-whelmed with relief. Life began to make sense; we began to see why the truth was important because it was the key to life! At that point, God brought a freedom and a joy to us almost like that of our salvation. I must say, Becky understood it first, she usually does, but we both finally saw what God was so desperately trying to show us. We became as bold as a Lion spiritually, and fear was exposed as a lie!

Over the following years, God was using what He had taught us to see not only *our* lives changed, but the lives of friends and fellow believers who were desperate and confused. The truth began to set free, marriages locked in abuse and turmoil. Truth began to release drug-addicted men and women from their servitude. Those bound by fear and shame were changed and released from the demons of strongholds. Why had we not discovered this earlier in our lives and ministry?

Becky and I often had our best times together dreaming and planning just before we would go to sleep. We would find ourselves sharing, with one another, and sometimes asking and answering questions. It was during one of those nights that the question was asked, "What is life really all about?" We, of course, knew the typical religious answers, but we pondered the question for maybe an hour and then we agreed to make it a matter of prayer and personal study until we felt that God had given us the answer.

For several weeks, we did our, own individual, digging, and praying about the question until one night we discovered that we had both come to the same conclusion based on the same scripture. It was John 14:6, "I am the way, and the truth, and the life; no one comes to the Father but through me."

There was an obvious meaning to the scripture, but God had led us both to a not so obvious conclusion, at least, not so obvious to us. God sent Jesus to be our Savior, and He was the path or the way to our salvation. We understood the fact that Jesus *is* the way, but it was the rest of the passage that revealed the answer we had been looking for.

The question that Becky and I had raised was, "What is LIFE really about?" It wasn't that we were not fulfilled or happy, but it was more about; are we accomplishing what God really desires for our lives? Can a person be happy or fulfilled if he is *not* accomplishing God's purpose? Some would argue, yes! I would argue no one can be fulfilled apart from God's purpose. I believe His purpose, whether we are religious or not, is what we must discover to genuinely experience life.

Where God began to focus our thoughts and concentration was on truth. Our question was about life, but God kept directing us back to the truth. As much as we wanted the answer to life, God relentlessly sent us back to the truth. "Ok, we get it, God! You want our focus to be on truth." We concluded that we needed to stop thinking about life, at least for the moment, and think about the direction God was trying to show us. "We want to know about life, but God, what do YOU want us to know?"

The key I've found to knowing God is to *listen* to Him! Just like little children, we have a lot of questions, but seldom have the patience and discipline to stop and listen.

So, we asked God, "What is it about TRUTH that you want us to know? Why should our focus be on truth when life is where we want to be?" I can honestly say, God is still revealing new information to us about truth, and it has been over fifteen years since we learned this principle!

Maybe our first clue should have been when we read John 18:37, "I have come into the world, to testify to the truth."

Even Jesus' focus was on truth. He wanted the world to know the truth, and that is still the case today. God's perspective on the world and the issues the world is facing politically, morally, and spiritually are vital.

Years after my salvation experience, I found myself still asking the question, "Where is the life?" As I mentioned, it was never a question of my relationship with the Lord or of my salvation which I had nailed down years before. Nor, did I doubt the indwelling of the Holy Spirit or feel the need for "more of Him." I think what I was experiencing was the pursuit of God. It was not *my* pursuit of Him, as much as *His* pursuit of me. He wanted me to "crawl up in His lap" and get to know Him. We all tend to get so busy that we ignore, or simply don't see, His pursuit for us.

It's been said so many times; seldom do we take the time to *listen!* We tend to do more talking and requesting than we do listening to God. This is especially hard for me. I am so active (ADHD) that for me to actually listen to God, it demands focus and concentration. It occasionally takes God, putting me on my back, or limiting my mobility just to help me listen to Him, as He did a few years ago while overseas. It was in China, on a medical trip, that I discovered a problem with blockage in an artery of my heart. It slowed me down drastically, and the doctors with me on the trip were very concerned. The event did, however, draw my attention back to hearing God.

So, what was God trying to show us? His revelation came as my wife, and I committed to fast and pray together until we heard from Him. God has many deep principles that He wants to teach us if we will just listen! My prayer is that you will learn this principle, which God so urgently wanted Becky and me to know, and that it will change your life as much as it has ours.

We began our search for truth, and little did we realize what God had in store for us. We never comprehended, at the time, how God would unfold the scripture to us, and how our listening to Him would amaze us!

This book comes out of a sincere and passionate desire for others to discover the truth about themselves and the world around them. If I could, I would scream it from every mountain top in the world, and to anyone who had even the slightest desire to listen!

The *Truth Principle* has revolutionized everything about us; the way we think, the way we feel, the way we interact, the way we pray, the way we choose, and the way we hear and receive. It has brought us confidence and peace in every area of our lives.

Becky said to me the other day, "I can't imagine *never* knowing these people!" She was referring to the small-town people in Texas, and a town to which we had recently moved. I had to agree with her; these people are wonderful!

I can't imagine *never* knowing the *Truth Principle!* Our lives before learning this principle were so drastically different. Not a day passes that we aren't reminded of the effect of what God has taught us through His truth.

Just recently, I traveled thirty minutes to the neighboring town of Amarillo, and a lady, eating in the restaurant there, told me how the *Truth Principle* changed her young suicidal sons' life. "He is now married and doing so well," she said. Our desire is for everyone to discover the *truth* for themselves.

Whether your understanding of truth is absolute or abstract, we are all looking for answers. The *Truth Principle* is what, I believe, will revolutionize anyone's life that is willing to stop and consider its significance.

I will first, examine the *Truth Principle* and the ten related pieces of the puzzle that God revealed to us, and secondly, in the final few chapters, I will address the truth concerning our world and families.

Don't allow my political and world observations in the final five chapters to draw you away from the *truth principle* itself, and the life change it can bring you. Your focus in the first ten or eleven chapters, and especially chapter three is critical for life change! The final five chapters are about world change, which is a natural conclusion to life change.

I will address world change, especially in chapter fifteen, when I expose the deliberate and systematic transformation that's focused on the millennial generation. What the socialist and humanist movement has invested in the next generation is shocking compared to the almost nonexistent effort by the conservative and Christian organizations! This must change!

My three sons are prolific songwriters and one song that Zach wrote, Hand of God says, "I see the hand of God in everything, and I'm not afraid 'Cause, the hand of God is holding on to me." That's exactly why <u>fear is a liar</u>!

"You will know the truth, and the truth will make you free!" (John 8:32)

TRUTH

Chapter 1: The Truth Principle

The problem begins in each of us and how we perceive ourselves. That perception might be molded by a poor home situation with endless screaming or ridicule and may even include physical abuse. Others may have had a stable home life but received a discouraging word or insult from a teacher or fellow classmate. The causes can be endless, but the results, in every case, can mold the perception of ourselves at least to some degree.

Some, for instance, can be very outgoing and even obnoxious to cover their genuine self-awareness of insecurity and shyness. Others will avoid groups or large gatherings because of their inaccurate perception of themselves when people sincerely enjoy their friendship.

We might observe people and believe they have it all together, when deep inside, they feel very inadequate.

Why do these thoughts of inadequacy or overconfidence continue to drive who we are? Why do we allow past hurts or abuses to shape who we are and discourage us? Why can't we just be ourselves and accept who we really are without the needless facades?

Let's be honest, we all have hurts or inadequacies that we wish could be revealed, but we dread the discovery of who we've become. What's needed is a "safe place" to unveil our true self, but where can we go for that "unveiling" without the consequences of our deception? We have created an image of ourselves, and to unpack that image is not an easy or pleasurable experience. This is where our battle for truth must begin; with ourselves, and with the reality that almost everyone else has some deep and humbling revelations to be unpacked as well.

We now live in a world that is running from the truth, when what's so desperately needed is that of running *to* the truth. Many people think; believing in truth and absolutes, leads to guilt and despair when the very opposite is the truth. They also believe if we just ignore or somehow decide that there is no real truth, then there will be no eventual consciences.

The believers of little or no absolutes will, on one hand, believe in physical absolutes like gravity, but on the other hand, deny there could be spiritual or even mental absolutes. My point is not to prove absolutes but to expand about truth as related to our lives.

Let's take the passage John 14:6 and examine it as have Becky and me over the past fifteen years.

"I am the way, and the truth, and the life; no one comes to the Father but through me."

What God began to show us was the "progression" of this passage, progressive in the sense of being connected or linked. God is the WAY, and we must go through TRUTH to get to LIFE! To proceed any other way but through truth to get to life, would leave us where many Christians settle, and that is just to know Christ only as of the way! If we are not living in truth, then the only logical conclusion would be that we are living a lie. Many might argue to live a good Christian life is not a lie, but I would argue that if we live any life, not in complete obedience and submission to Christ, it is a disobedient life!

Jeremiah 29:11-13 points out the problem very clearly. "For I know the plans that I have for you,' declares the Lord, 'plans for welfare and not for calamity to give you a future and a hope. Then you will call upon Me and come and pray to Me, and I will listen to you. You will seek Me and find Me when you search for Me with all your heart."

We find ourselves immersed in *our* plans and *our* activities rather than in the plans that God has for us. Can we be doing many "good things?" YES, but are we doing the things that God desires for us to do?

When Jesus called the disciples, He told them to "leave father and mother and follow me!" To the rich young ruler, He declared to him, "sell all that you have and come follow me."

It is not a reality that we might be doing many "good things" that brings little temporary satisfaction or pleasure, but it's *God's* plan that brings the true fulfillment and accomplishment that we all need.

Someone recently shared an experience that I believe illustrates this point perfectly. A father, one night, at the supper table had mentioned the necessity for the trim on the house to be painted, but he was going on a business trip the following day. After supper, the father asked his two sons to "please clean up your rooms before I return home tomorrow night!" As the father arrived back home from the business trip and drove up to the house, to his pleasure, he saw the sons painting the trim. The father expressed his delight to the boys only to find out later, that their rooms were still in disarray and had not been cleaned as he had requested.

We can be achieving many "good things," but are we accomplishing what the Father has asked us to do? Are we "painting the trim" when we should be cleaning our rooms?

The passage goes on to mention calamity. Calamity, amid doing *God's* will, becomes an opportunity as in the case of Joseph when his brothers sold him into slavery. As a result, Joseph became an administrator over all of Egypt. Calamity, amid doing *our* will, or our "good things," becomes an encumbrance and only adds to our already substantial load.

Maybe our disobedience is not a conscious choice, but rather a routine choice. We are good people, trying to do "the right thing." The routine kicks in because we get up, shower, go to work, and do our church activities on schedule. The problem comes when we neglect to consult God on his plan for us that day.

My day usually starts in the shower by asking God, "What do you have for me today, God? To whom is it that I need to minister and see today? What is it that you want to teach me, God, and what is it about me that you choose to change or adjust? God, give me Divine appointments, and open and close doors that are of you, and not me. Make me a clean instrument, available and open to your direction today!"

I am convinced that most Christians never discover or even know *how* to discover their *purpose in life*. It was *never* in God's plan for us to guess His will, and to hope in the end, that we would accomplish that for which we were created.

God's word, throughout both the Old and New Testament, guides us over seventy times to purpose, and more specifically, to God's purpose for us!

"Not that I have already obtained *it* or have already become perfect, but I press on so that I may lay hold of that for which I was also laid hold of by Christ Jesus. Brethren, I do not regard myself as having laid hold of *it* yet; but one thing I do: forgetting what lies behind and reaching forward to what lies ahead, I press on toward the goal for the prize of the upward call of God in Christ Jesus." (Philippians 3:12-14)

This passage doesn't mention purpose specifically, but it does emphasize our need to "lay hold" of God's call; to forget the past and focus on His call for *us*!

The following passages are a sample of New Testament scriptures that do refer specifically to purpose.

"And we know that God causes all things to work together for good to those who love God, to those who are called according to *His* purpose." (Romans 8:28)

"For David, after he had served the purpose of God in his own generation, fell asleep, and was laid among his fathers…" (Acts 13:36)

"Now He who prepared us for this very purpose is God, who gave to us the Spirit as a pledge." (2 Corinthians 5:5)

"For this purpose, also I labor, striving according to His power, which mightily works within me." (Colossians 1:29)

"Or do you think the scripture speaks to no purpose: "He jealously desires the Spirit which He made to dwell in us." (James 4:5)

"Not returning evil for evil or insult for insult but giving a blessing instead; for you were called for the very purpose that you might inherit a blessing." (1 Peter 3:9)

God wants to fulfill His purpose in us. Not only does God's purpose include sharing salvation through faith in Jesus Christ His Son, but more specifically, God has a plan and an assignment. That assignment is for every Christian to accomplish, by the power of the Holy Spirit who lives within each one of us, as God's children! So, let's explore for a moment, what your purpose might be.

What is it that brings you pleasure and fulfillment...the thing that you really enjoy doing? Knowing the answer to this question is the first step to discovering your *purpose in life*. For me, it is *connecting* people to discover new truths for the first time. I love teaching what God has taught me. My joy comes from learning a principle, but then, helping someone else experience that principle for themselves, and that is what brings me fulfillment. It could be from the first time I helped someone learn to solve a problem in their life, to speaking to a large group and seeing light bulbs go on. I will never forget the first individual whom I personally led to the Lord; it *literally* saved her life! And the times in China when I shared Christ with people who had never before heard the name Jesus, life-changing! I love *connecting*!

What are you passionate about? What is it that others may find as work, but that you find fulfilling? Consider your passion, and then ask God if that might be a clue to your purpose. Many famous sports figures have taken the passion for their sport and have used it as an opportunity and a platform to share Christ. Others have taken their wealth and have financed organizations to support orphanages or the disadvantaged. Maybe your passion is writing, or cooking, or traveling, or building; whatever that passion may be, it could very well connect God's purpose for your life.

My daily prayer: "Search me, O God, and know my heart; Try me and know my anxious thoughts; and see if there be any harmful way in me, and lead me in the everlasting way." (Psalm 139:23-24)

Our service to God cannot be routine "good things," but needs to be active and changing. We should anticipate that; at any moment or in any situation, God is working, and He may want to work through us in that instant.

Several years ago, a computer tech told me to save my work often. He said, "Anytime you think about it, SAVE!" I "save" routinely now, but it wasn't until after my computer shut down and I lost one hours-worth of work, that couldn't be retrieved, that I began to save!

As intent as I am to "save" my computer work, I need to be that intent and alert to confessing my sin and disobedience. Then, I need to focus on what God wants to do in, thru, and around me today! Can you imagine what God could accomplish if every Christian was that intent and deliberate in their walk with Christ? We can't be responsible for every Christian, but we are responsible for ourselves!

This is entirely an assumption, but I believe that many well-meaning Christians, who attended church regularly, have raised good kids, and volunteered for church and community projects may find, when they get to heaven, that "they placed their ladder on the wrong wall." They may find that God's plan for them was entirely different from that of their own personal schedule. What's important is the truth! I believe for each Christian there is a truth and a lie, a purpose, or just an existence.

My prayer is that the Church will wake up out of their existence and seek the truth. The result will be LIFE! This principle will not only awaken Christians to life, but it also sets captives free. I will attempt to explain and illustrate how both can be accomplished when the *principle of truth* is applied and followed.

As Christians, as the Church, we were designed to impact the world outside of the "Church!"

In over one hundred-thirty passages and sixteen books of the New Testament, Jesus referenced the "Kingdom of

Heaven" or "Kingdom of God." God's plan for us is bigger than just our salvation, and it incorporates His Kingdom!

I will elaborate further on this point, but the "world" has figured this out. The world is not afraid to venture outside their realm and go into another, maybe uncomfortable, domain to expand their philosophy! The Church, for years, has expected the world to come to them, and to adjust to them, but the church finds it uncomfortable going into the world and its culture. An example would be the gay and lesbian culture "coming out" and systematically reaching not just their base, but the seven cultural areas of influence: the worlds of entertainment, government, education, media, business, traditional families, and now even the religious world!

If the Church would follow the command of Christ and "go unto all the world," as have the rest of our culture then, we might well see a different outcome than we are seeing now. I will elaborate more on the seven cultural areas of influence in chapter fifteen.

During my traveling years, I was awakened to the fact that all churches were not the same, and truth was expressed in different ways. My twin brother and I had been in all "brands" of churches. My wife compares it to the personality tests similar to Myers Briggs, that most of us have taken before. Some tests use colors others use animals but I'm going to use the traditional ancient Greek terms for sake of illustration.

The **Sanguine**, or outgoing personality, she assigned to our Pentecostal brothers and sisters. They are the life of the party in the church world, never a dull moment. The **Choleric,** or strong-willed achievers would be my Baptist friends. They certainly aren't the life of the party, but they excel in organizing the party. The **Melancholic** or analytical brethren are represented by the Bible churches. Accuracy is very important, and the pros and cons of the party were no doubt discussed. Finally, there are the **Phlegmatic** or laid back non-denominational churches. These are very easy going, coffee drinking, relaxed churches that enjoy the party and stay to the end.

My analogy may be oversimplified, and certainly not intended to offend any denomination, but Becky's point was that not any one church could stake a claim on all truth. Each church exhibited some of the truth, in unique ways and all the personalities are needed. The result was that we learned something valuable from each church. We saw strengths and weaknesses in each "brand" of the church, but the most important lesson was the truth that we learned from each part of the body of Christ.

One day the Church will wake up and say, "Why weren't we more like the church at Acts? They had all things in common and loved one another." That awakening will only come when we seek truth and not tradition. Tradition is not wrong, and in many ways is very good, unless it undermines truth and exalts itself. Of that, we need to be very careful.

There is truth; physical, mental, and spiritual. There is truth for the Church and truth for the individual. When the individual finds, accepts, and practices truth, the Church will begin to be what God intended for it to be. I'm not responsible for others, I'm responsible for me.

After all my experiences, in childhood, from traveling and pastoring, it was refreshing to finally discover freedom. All that I had learned and experienced began to make sense when I discovered the *principle of truth.*

"...and you will know the truth, and the truth will make you free." (John 8:32)

I pointed out earlier that the *Truth Principle* is progressive; "I am the way, the truth, and the life!" (John 14:6)

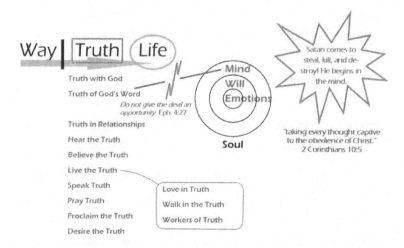

We move from the <u>way</u> (knowing Christ as Savior)

through <u>truth</u> (God's Word) to discover <u>life</u> (God's purpose).

The illustration will explain and give a visual road map of the *truth principle* that God revealed to Becky and me. Life is our goal, but we cannot bypass the *truth* to arrive there.

God revealed several aspects of truth to us and continues to do so as we listen and respond obediently to Him.

I will break down and explain each step of the *Truth Principle* in the following chapters: Truth with God, Truth of God's Word, Truth in Relationships, Hear the Truth, Believe the Truth, Live the Truth, Speak the Truth, Pray the Truth, Proclaim the Truth, and Desire the Truth.

Please don't allow this limited, incomplete, sample to restrict what God wants to teach and reveal to you about this unfinished, and life-changing principle of Truth.

He continues to teach us more each day and you will learn even more concepts of truth as you allow the Holy Spirit to reveal His unique work in you.

Chapter 2: Truth with God

The first characteristic of truth is *truth with God*. It involves a vertical relationship with God. We sometimes assume that God is God, and consequently, He already knows everything about us past, present, and future. He *does* already know everything about us, but He wants us to confess, or acknowledge that which He already knows.

As parents, we have all experienced the disobedience of our children and hiding the offense from us. Even though we are aware of their concealed deed, we will give them a chance to own up to it and seek forgiveness.

I remember one of our children driving our car while we were away from the house for a few minutes. He was fifteen at the time, so he knew full well the implication of his behavior. When we returned home, something told me to touch the hood of the car (hearing God!) I reached out, and as I moved closer, I heard the engine popping and cooling down. Sure enough, the hood was hot, so I assumed it had been driven longer than just around the block.

Becky and I entered the house and immediately summoned Matthew, whom we suspicioned to be the guilty party. "Matthew," I said, 'where did you take the car?" A surprised and guilt-ridden look filled his face. "Aaa, I didn't take it anywhere," he said. After a little back and forth, and him finally realizing he had been exposed, Matthew eventually confessed and expressed his sincere regret for the act. (It wasn't all that simple, but I'll leave it at that)

We do nothing apart from the knowledge of God. He is not seeking to discover our sin but desires for us to admit our sin and repent of it. He already knows the truth, and he wants us to admit the truth to Him so our relationship with Him, may be restored.

We are saints and no longer sinners! Our sin, past, present, and future was paid for. The Bible says, "we are the righteousness of God!" Ephesians 6:14 (KJV)

In speaking to "believers," Paul makes his address to the "saints" in Romans, Corinthians, Ephesians, Philippians, Colossians, and other Bible books and not to the sinners!

Canonization is admirable when recognizing deceased members of distinction in the Catholic Church, but

Sainthood is given to each "believer," and bestowed by God through Christ's shed blood on the cross, at the time of one's salvation. Pastors or priests cannot impart one's sainthood!

Colossians 3:1 Speaking to Christians, says, "Therefore if you have been raised with Christ, keep seeking the things above, where Christ is, seated at the right hand of God."

To quote Paul Burleson, with whom I was on staff in Oklahoma, "We have been co-resurrected, co-ascended and co-seated in heavenly places with Christ Jesus, our Lord!"

My son Matthew, no matter what he does, will never lose the love of his father. He will always be my son, and nothing can change that fact. However, our relationship can sometimes be strained, and when it is, admitting ones' faults and shortcomings will always mend a true unconditional relationship. God will "never leave us or forsake us" when we have received Him as Savior. But our relationship can sometimes be strained because of our disobedience.

So, the first step under truth is *truth with God*. Take the time to be open and honest with God. Nothing we've done is unknown to God, nor will it ever take Him by surprise! His love will never alter or change toward us at all! In fact, the greater sin, if there is one, is that of disobedience to God, and pretending innocent. Every sin we've committed or ever will commit, past, present, and future was paid for on the cross over two thousand years ago. God is a just and loving God, compassionate and understanding, caring, and full of grace. He chose to give His life on the cross so the debt for our sin would be paid in full! Why would we be afraid to be truthful with Him?

I will admit that sometimes I feel shame when approaching God, but He has never been less than gracious and kind in His response to me. Yes, He will discipline me, but it will always be from the hand of a loving and gracious Father.

Our fear of God may come from an inappropriate response to our earthly father. I am certainly guilty of that with my own children, just ask them. But over the years, and as my parenting skills improved, I developed the ability to discipline out of love, not anger, to step back take a deep breath and handle each situation responsibly. God will always handle discipline responsibly.

Our fear may also come because we haven't taken the time to get to know God and to build our side of the relationship with Him. This may sound odd to you, but I have found that God has a sense of humor and that he wants to enjoy our time with Him. The name Yahweh (I Am Who I Am) was a name for God that men in Old Testament times were afraid to speak. As a result, Adonai was used but had a much different meaning, Lord, or Master. I will elaborate more about Adonai in a moment.

Yahweh (I Am Who I Am) was a personal name; much like a friend named William would be when asking us to call him Bill. The idea was that God wanted to have a close personal relationship, a more relaxed and engaging connection with us. God wanted to be approachable. This made the religious rulers of the time uncomfortable, so they chose a more distant and detached association with God. They felt it was disrespectful to call Him Yahweh, yet God was seeking a more personal loving relationship. Therefore, "Kingdom of Heaven" was used out of respect in the book of Matthew twenty-six times as opposed to "Kingdom of God," mentioned only twice when Jesus introduced the phrase. Most of the other New Testament books used "Kingdom of God" almost exclusively, as a more casual response.

Today, God still desires to be Yahweh in our life. He wants to draw close and know us, and He wants us to know Him in a personal and more intimate way, just like we would want with a good friend. The problem is that we, much like the religious leaders, assume that God is unattainable or distant and that we are unworthy to have a first name relationship with Him. This is untrue, but we continue to believe it.

When my children were young, I remember them coming into our bedroom, in the early mornings, and jumping on the bed to wrestle and pillow fight. I still have this tradition with our eleven grandchildren; we call it "roughhousing." I will hear their childish giggles, as they quietly (not really) open the door and slowly creep in until unleashing their pillows on me. We could do this for hours if time allowed. The fun part about it for me is to grab and tickle them and kiss their cold, chubby little cheeks.

I remember meeting an elderly Chinese man who practiced the Dongba religion. Dongba's are Pantheists; they believe that nature is God. I had built a relationship with Mr. Hé over several years of going to China, and I was sitting in his home one day drinking green tea.

He was explaining to me a painting on his wall saying, that Dongba's prayed to nature, mountains, rivers, trees, and the sky. I asked why he didn't pray to God directly and he explained that he believed there was a God, but that man could not speak directly to Him. As I began to describe God's sending of His son to die for us, and that God did want to personally communicate to him, and have a relationship with him, he began to cry. Mr. Hé said to me, "Do you mean that I have been praying to mountains all my life when I could have been praying directly to God?" I responded, "Yes Mr. Hé, you have been 'worshiping the creation rather than the Creator!'" He was so excited, about knowing the truth, that he grabbed me and my interpreter by the hand, and wanted us to tell the rest of his family, and other friends in the village. Mr. Hé, for the first time in his life, began to enjoy a *personal* relationship with God.

God isn't going to "rough house" with us, but he does enjoy His time with us. I think that which He likes most is when we meet with Him in the morning, and we just allow Him to hold us and love us.

When we get to know this side of God, we anticipate our times together, and we allow correction more easily. He is not creation, He is Creator, and we are His creation whom He loves.

Take the first step in your journey to life; be truthful with God and tell Him what He already knows. His response will always be from the heart of a loving father, and in time, the meetings will be that of anticipation and excitement of learning from Him.

This step will begin the freedom and purpose everyone is looking for and have desired for so long.

Truth with God

TRUTH

Chapter 3: Truth of God's Word

The second characteristic, the *Truth of God's Word*, is the step that excites me most of all. This step is the most fundamental and essential message of the book, and one that will change lives, and set the captives free!

I have shared this step of the Truth Principle, with hundreds of people including drug addicts, alcoholics, gossips, and control fanatics. This principle has freed many with sexual strongholds such as pornography, lust, and homosexuality. Those with anger issues, fear, and suicidal thoughts have been liberated and their lives, and families have been restored. All, without exception, came willing and seeking solutions to their questions.

Many have said they never realized the source of their condition but knew that something was wrong and that they'd never considered that a solution was possible. Some sought psychological counseling with little or no deliverance from their struggle until learning the *truth principle*, and discovered that their fight was not psychological, but spiritual!

I don't want to minimize the help that many psychiatrists and physicians have given to remedy people of medical and psychological ills. However, our medical world seldom considers the spiritual aspect of a problem, when the root cause could, in many cases, be spiritual. In fact, I have counseled many whose problems were exacerbated because a drug or procedure was given just trying to alleviate the symptoms of what turned out to be spiritual, rather than physical or psychological. I appreciate the doctor who will refer a patient to counseling before prescribing something which may or may not help but might only mask the source rather than reveal it.

Several years ago, in San Antonio, my brother was called to a psychiatric hospital to help with an overpowering patient with whom the doctors had reached an impasse. At the request of the patient, Phil went to the hospital. The psychiatrists asked permission to remain in the room with Phil and the patient. After Phil dealt with the problem from the spiritual perspective, and the doctor saw the positive result, and he admitted not knowing how to handle similar circumstances, especially from the spiritual perspective. Phil was later able to meet with the psychiatrist to explain what he had done, but more importantly, what God had done through him!

As I expound on this stage of truth; *Truth of God's Word*, I will include testimonies of those with whom I have personally met and have followed over their course of recovery. I will change the names for privacy purposes, and out of respect for the individuals.

Over my forty-eight years in the ministry, I have encountered many people with the strongholds that I have described. The interesting fact is, that even though the strongholds varied, the solution seldom changed. God's Word is true!

"For the word of God is living and active and sharper than any two-edged sword, and piercing as far as the division of soul and spirit, of both joints and marrow, and able to judge the thoughts and intentions of the heart." (Hebrews 4:12)

Satan hates God's Word! When we petition the Word of God against our strongholds, Satan and His demons must leave! Okay, I need to explain before everyone starts having visions of *The Exorcists*, and heads turning around three hundred and sixty degrees.

Satan is factual, and I believe every battle we have whether personal, congregational, or political is instigated or encouraged by Satan. Yes, I know some of the pain we experience is initiated by our personal choices, but don't think for a moment that Satan doesn't seize the opportunity to complicate and exacerbate a poor choice on our part. Folks, we are in a battle here! Any good fighter will look for an opening and a chance for an advantage. Satan is the ultimate fighter, deceiver, and conspirator, and he is "seeking whom he may devour!" (1 Peter 5:8)

Strongholds begin with open doors. If we open a door to any sin, it will multiply and develop from our thought or action, into a full and mature stronghold. If we allow it, the action can move from a thought in our *mind,* to us *willfully* acting on that thought, and the thought eventually becomes an *emotional* stronghold. (*See ill. Page 34*) A stronghold is not demon possession, but rather a territory given over by the believer, whereby Satan steals what isn't his, and manipulates it! Demon possession, however, is that of Satan possessing what is already his! When one doesn't know Christ as Savior, nothing is there to impede Satan's possession of them if he chooses.

For the believer, Satan's battlefield is the mind! Just fewer than two hundred scriptures include the word mind, and most mention the flesh or Satan, and our human struggles in that area. The mind is the door to the **soul** (mind, will, and emotions) so it is important to guard the *door*!

That's why 2 Corinthians 10:5 commands us to "take every thought captive to the obedience of Christ!"

"For I joyfully concur with the law of God in the inner man, but I see a different law in the members of my body, waging war against the law of my *mind* and making me a prisoner of the law of sin which is in my members. Wretched man that I am! Who will set me free from the body of this death? Thanks be to God through Jesus Christ our Lord! So then, on the one hand, I myself with my *mind* am serving the law of God, but on the other, with my flesh the law of sin." (Romans 7:22-25)

The problem multiplies when we allow a thought to move from our *mind* and *willfully* invite strongholds into our LIVING ROOM (*emotions*)! We have all experienced guests in our homes that will not leave! Strongholds will not only stay as well, but they will also set up camp, they will put down stakes, and they will resist any effort to remove them except the truth!

To open the door of our *mind* to strongholds and allow them to *willfully* pass into our *emotions* or "living room," will eventually become uncontrolled anger, lust, gossip, fear, control, rejection, loneliness, unforgiveness, depression, and any unwelcomed manifestation that then becomes hostile to leaving, and digs in its unrestrained heels, taking on the form of a habit or stronghold!

The human being is made of body, soul, and spirit. It is in the body and soul where we *allow* strongholds to establish a foothold and live! The spirit is where the Holy Spirit abides and gives us morals, values, and a sense of right or wrong. Strongholds can't exist there!

A young man, we will call Raymond, found his anger out of control. It was affecting his marriage and family, and even causing problems on the job. Raymond scheduled a time to meet with me and included his wife in the meeting. As our appointment progressed, we discovered that Raymond's anger began as a young boy. His father provoked him regularly even taunting him because he was "too soft." As Raymond grew, so did his anger. He said that it started slowly but as it progressed, he found it to be out of control and would express his anger even under the calmest of circumstances.

The largest percent of our learning comes between the ages of birth to eight years old (80%). During that time, we have already developed a perception of ourselves. Most often, that perception, good or bad, has been stimulated by those around us. It's usually not until our teenage years or later, that we begin the struggle with whatever our identity has become, and we then desire to find answers.

"...be angry, and yet do not sin; do not let the sun go down on your anger, and do not give the devil an opportunity." (Ephesians 4:26-27)

Consider anger for a moment. We can all find those moments of anger in our lives. When those moments come, and they will, we have a choice. We can allow that anger to manifest and then act it out, or we can "take that thought captive to the obedience of Christ," (2 Corinthians 10:5) and stop the anger in our mind. The stronghold only matures when we allow that anger to move from our *mind* to our *will* (where we willfully choose to be angry) and then we allow this process to happen again and again without "taking the thoughts captive." If not stopped, it will eventually move to our *emotions* (if we allow it) and will develop into a demonic stronghold! My wife likes to picture taking the thought and holding it out where she can see it. Then she speaks to fear or anger and commands it to be gone in the Name of Jesus, and by the shed blood of Jesus!

The thought is taken captive by choosing not to act on it, and then applying the truth, or the word of God that speaks to that particular thought. The "thought" could be anger, lust, gossip, fear, or any number of temptations that need to have corresponding scripture applied. I have included examples of strongholds and corresponding scriptures at the end of this chapter.

Fear is another stronghold. We've all known of people who live in fear to the extent that they hear voices or assumes that everyone is some sort of enemy, and they live in a constant state of paranoia. Many times, treatment will only mask and sometimes enhance the true source of the problem with only prescriptions or ineffective medicinal management. One must always consider a spiritual stronghold as a possible source of fear.

The tabernacle is the perfect picture of this process. The tabernacle is designed with three basic rooms: The Outer Court (body), the Holy Place (soul), and the Holy of Holies (Spirit). Although Christians cannot be demon-possessed, we *can* open ourselves to demonic strongholds in our flesh (body), and in our <u>mind</u>, <u>will</u>, and <u>emotions</u> (soul). Our *spirit* is, of course, where the Holy Spirit dwells, and only the Spirit! The Apostle Paul spoke openly in Galatians of our need as Christians to die to our flesh.

The three rooms of the tabernacle can have many symbols: *cleansing* in the outer court, or "sacrifice," *communion* in the holy place, or "tent of meeting" and *completion* in the holy of holies. These are three parallels that are sometimes used to illustrate: *body*, *soul*, and *Spirit*.

When approaching God with our strongholds, we come <u>sacrificing</u> our pride and our will, and restoring our relationship with God by <u>communicating</u>, and finally experiencing that freedom and release which comes only after we know all is forgiven and redeemed, <u>completion</u>.

What exactly is "taking a thought captive?" The only spiritual step we can take while in the flesh is to surrender and willingly allow God to work. Satan, unlike God, only hears our spoken words not our thoughts, so taking a thought captive needs to be done audibly, "Anger, (lust, gossip, and control) in the name of Jesus, and by His shed blood on the cross, you are defeated!" Jesus and His blood are our only authority against Satan except for the Word of God, so *always* apply and speak scripture when confronting any stronghold.

I remember teenagers coming into my office saying, "I can't do anything right!" My response would be, "that's a lie from Satan!" Then I would say, "The Bible says, 'I can do all things through Christ who strengthens me.' (Philippians 4:13) That's the truth!"

I would hear people say, "I can't go on." I would say, "my grace is sufficient!' (2 Corinthians 12:9) "That's the truth!"

Others would say, "I'm afraid." I would respond, "God says, 'I have not given you the spirit of fear.' (2 Timothy 1:7) that's the truth!"

Too often, people will believe a lie from Satan and not the *truth of God's word!*

It is important to not only discover the lie but to ask God to reveal to you the source of the lie. Was it from an experience as a child; maybe abuse or rejection, or did a teacher, as in my case, publicly embarrass you? Each lie has a source and a beginning, and God wants us to know the origin, and to activate the healing from that point.

On several occasions, I would hear people say, "I'm ugly or I'm not pretty." My response would be, "So you think God is ugly? Because God says, 'we are created in His image." (Genesis 1:27)

"The thief (Satan) comes to steal, kill and destroy" (John 10:10) and he begins in the mind, convincing us that we are ugly, or fearful, or hopeless, or inadequate, or angry, or unworthy...fill in the blank! These are all lies from Satan! "God comes that we might have *life* and have it more *abundantly!*"

My wife and I have adopted a motto, "What is the truth about that?" Underline that quote, memorize it, mark it down, and use it often! I can't emphasize this point enough! One will encounter lies daily, maybe even hourly, and when we do, we *must* examine them for truth!

Even in the Church, lies are disseminated. Some of the most common lies in the Church are, "you need to dress your best." What is the truth about that? God's word says, "For man looks at the outward appearance, but God looks at the heart." (1 Samuel 15:7) Another lie in the Church is, "we need to sing only hymns!" What is the truth about that? "Praise Him with Hymns and songs and spiritual songs. (Ephesians 5:19) Praise Him with timbre and harp and loud-sounding cymbals." (Psalm 149-150) Yes, it is true, we do need to sing hymns, but our praise is not limited to hymns, which is sometimes the inference when that statement is made. Singing choruses and praises are scriptural, complaining about them is sin! Many times, we need to ask, "What is the truth about that," concerning our traditions in the Church. I believe traditions are very important, but not at the expense of truth!

I remember during my youth ministry days that tradition was important when it came to camp. Because we attended the same camp for fifteen years, many of the students wanted to return every year. It was not difficult to motivate our students to attend that camp. However, I had to be willing to adjust that camp tradition as I moved to a different staff assignment and gave way to a new student minister. He had a new vision for what camp should be for his students. When it came to the new camp, I asked myself, "What is the truth about that?" I could not honestly find any scriptural reason to hold on to my tradition, so I didn't! We must ask ourselves, "Are our traditions about God, or are they just about us?" The latter is a sin.

We have mentioned many strongholds in this chapter, anger, gossip, lust, control, fear, depression, suicide, addictions, and others. One with which I have never struggled is homosexuality. Homosexuality is a struggle for many, and I do not want to demean or degrade those who deal with this lifestyle. We will probably never agree together on this issue and its difficult territories of debate, but my love for the wonderful people of this lifestyle is great, and I believe my friends who have chosen this path will confirm my love for them. I mention it only because I have placed a roadblock up in the area of this temptation. Placing that roadblock is easy for me to do because I have never had any desire or temptation in this area at all. I do not understand the desire for homosexuality, but many do, and for them, there is no roadblock. I am sure my LGBT friends don't agree that this is a stronghold, and disregards scripture, but I lovingly ask them to consider, "what is the truth about that?"

My point is that we find it easy to put roadblocks up in areas where *we* have no struggles, but why are we unwilling to place roadblocks in those areas where we surrender so easily such as anger, lust, or gossip?

To place a roadblock is being willing to say, "What is the truth about that?" If indeed there is a truth to be followed, why then are we so reluctant to examine that truth? "You will know the truth, and the truth will make you free." (John 8:32)

Since learning this principle, it is sometimes difficult to understand why people don't want the life, freedom, and completion that it brings. We should always be willing to question our beliefs in search of the truth.

I've seen people who were homeless begging for every scrap of food possible just to live. I've seen them sheltered under a piece of cardboard while lying on a snow-covered sidewalk, just struggling to stay warm. Why would *anyone* refuse a job or an opportunity to live in a warm place, with the prospect of eating good meals every day? It baffles me that those living on the street would refuse that offer, but they do! I have presented lifestyle change and good jobs to such people only to be told, "No." I don't understand that, and I never will. But it is hard to comprehend, as well, why someone will refuse to put roadblocks in areas of their lives that only bring strongholds, destruction, and defeat. I'm guilty! I have done it many times as well. But, with God's help and direction I have learned to place those roadblocks where they need to be. I'm not perfect, but my life has drastically changed, and I am making much better choices than before, since learning the *truth principle*.

Again, the *truth of God's Word*. The Bible is the standard, and it's not whatever we choose the standard to be. It has stood the test for over 2,000 years despite a concerted effort to change, silence, and destroy its message. Every year, additional evidence is discovered which only proves more and more of God's word to be the true, infallible document God said it is.

At this point, I feel it is important to share another person's major struggle. The young lady has allowed me to convey her story openly in the past, but I am choosing not to reveal her name in this context even though God has done such a miracle in her life. Her story was the motivation for the title of this book, Fear is a Liar! I believe fear is one of the stoutest strongholds, and most difficult to overcome.

At the time of the first manifested struggle with her stronghold, I had only known the family maybe one or two years. It was during camp at our first morning worship, when a group of five or six high school girls came in the chapel crying, supping, and bellowing to me about Katy. They had been up-all-night crying with her and really didn't know why. We went outside of the chapel to talk, and I began asking her questions. It was hard to even communicate at first because of the intense emotion, but as she began to settle down a little, my only conclusion was that she was homesick. Her dad was at the camp as a sponsor and was on his way up from the cafeteria to meet us. Katy agreed with her dad and me to stay one more night and see if things got better. If there wasn't improvement by the next morning, we would call her mother to come to get her.

The next morning was like groundhog day. All the girls were again upset, and we were unable to resolve the problem or even get close to what the root cause might be. Katy's mom drove the seven hours from Texas to Colorado to pick up her daughter but was too tired to turn around and return home that afternoon. Again, even having her mom in the dorm with her, Katy could not resolve the problem. Wednesday morning at breakfast, Katy was still showing signs of a rough night even though she would be going home very shortly.

Her parents and I agreed to meet the next week after camp and see if we could discern Katy's struggle under more normal circumstances. The days leading to our appointment were filled with much prayer and fasting as we sought God for answers.

Our appointment was just several months after God had taught Becky and me the *principle of truth*. I knew that God had given me this principle for times such as this, and indeed He had!

On the day of the appointment, Katy's mother had to work but her dad and I met with her the Monday following camp. I began the session in prayer and asked Katy to share any insight that she might have learned over the four days since returning home. She really didn't have any specific answers, so I began asking questions.

Even though I had only known the family for about two years, I felt that I knew them well because they were very faithful and involved in our ministry.

After some basic questions with no real triggers forthcoming, God prompted me to ask a question that I really didn't want to ask. I had learned from past experience that fear, this intense, came many times from abuse. I knew before we ever met that day, that Katy's struggle had to be deeper and more involved than just homesickness. Katy's dad offered to step outside if she preferred to answer the question privately, but she wanted her dad there. "Katy," I said, "Have you ever been abused?" Quickly her dad said, "No, of course not!" But Katy quietly answered, "Yes, I have." She began struggling through the story of being abused by a doctor after a sports injury at another camp several years earlier. Katy had kept this occurrence to herself for numerous years until that day in my office.

As a result, after a couple of hours, we were able to pinpoint the stronghold of fear in Katy's life. Fear, in my opinion, is one of the most resilient demonic strongholds one can experience. We researched several scriptures on fear that day which I challenged Katy to memorize. I then showed Katy and her dad how to scripturally defeat that "spirit of fear!" (2 Timothy 1:7) We first quoted the scriptures out loud (we wanted the enemy to hear them) then I had Katy repeat a prayer with me; "Fear, in the name of Jesus, and by the blood of Jesus, you are defeated! You have no authority over me, and you must leave, and go to the pit of hell!" Satan's demons adopt the names of strongholds and therefore, are addressed directly in the prayer. They are free to enter someone else, or even an animal unless ordered into hell.

As I mentioned earlier, I believe the stronghold of fear is one of the strongest, and it was boldly displaying itself in Katy's instance. It was a relief to finally discover the source. Katy's dad tried to locate the doctor in question but because of time and relocation was regrettably unable to resolve that end of the conflict.

Katy suggested over the next few weeks that everything was going better, and at any indication that her struggle with fear was about to reemerge, she would verbally quote the scriptures and take authority over the stronghold of fear. Neither Katy nor her parents mentioned any struggles unless, in their words, "minor" occurrences might arise, but they were feeling very good about her progress.

About one month later, Katy was signed up to attend a Super Summer event with several of our students, in Abilene, Texas which was about six hours from home. I communicated with Katy and her parents before going but had a peace that she was ready for the challenge. We got to Abilene that afternoon in time for registration and dinner with six or seven hundred other students at the campus cafeteria. I didn't see Katy again until right before the evening worship was about to begin. Katy came running up to me with fear in her eyes, obviously panicked and asking to go home. I explained that we couldn't leave right then, but we prayed and went through the steps of authority together. Then, I told her to go with her group to the balcony and that I would talk to her after the service. Katy reluctantly languished up the steps to her age group, as I went with my group to the main floor, while asking God for a miracle!

The speaker that week was Louie Giglio, and as he got up to speak he announced his message title as "Fear." I turned and looked up at the balcony to find Katy, and our eyes met immediately! I mouthed to her, "Listen!" I knew she would. This, no doubt, was a Divine appointment!

After about forty minutes, Louie prayed and gave an invitation. I turned to look at Katy, and with a huge smile on her face she mouthed to me, "It's GONE!" As soon as the service was dismissed Katy and I found one another and had a BIG hug and crying session together!

Since that day, I am proud to say that Katy went with me to China on a trip and has since been to Cambodia and Africa on three-year mission stints. She came back home and finished seminary and is now in India as a career Southern Baptist missionary! She told me recently that there will be times that fear will try to battle back, but she will take authority in Jesus' name, and everything will be fine.

I mentioned *Adonai* earlier. *Adonai* means lordship, surrender, and Master. This is the objective that God has for us, not just the physical or emotional healing, but us, releasing all that we are, to all that He is. That's when real and true healing comes. *Yahweh Rophe* denotes complete healing; Greek word *iaomai* (deliverance) in our mind, will and emotion, and occurs when we *Adonai*, surrender! Don't settle for incomplete healing but surrender to the healing God wants to give us that will bring total and complete *freedom!*

"But each one is tempted when he is carried away and enticed by his own lust. Then when lust has conceived, it gives birth to sin; and when sin is accomplished, it brings forth death." (James 1:14-15)

This passage illustrates, again, the three steps; Mind, Will, and Emotions. We are enticed by Satan in our Mind, it is conceived in our willful act, and it brings death to our Emotions in the form of a demonic stronghold.

The truth of God's word is important and should be used at the door of our mind anytime we are tempted. We need to learn to recognize the lie and apply the truth of God's word. Don't believe the lie, believe the truth!

I have listed ten samples on the next two pages of truth as opposed to a lie. This is an example of the importance to memorize and apply scripture.

You say: "I can't do it"
God says: "You can do all things"
(Philippians 4:13)

You say: "I'm ugly"
God says: "in the image of God He created you"
(Genesis 1:26-27)

You say: "It's impossible"
God says: "All things are possible"
(Luke 18:27)

You say: "I'm too tired"
God says: "I will give you rest"
(Matthew 11:28-30)

You say: "No one really loves me"
God says: "I love you"
(John 3:16)

You say: "I can't go on"
God says: "My grace is sufficient"
(II Corinthians 12:9 & Psalm 91:15)

You say: "I can't forgive myself"
God says: "I Forgive you"
(I John 1:9 & Romans 8:1)

You say: "I'm afraid"
God says: "I have not given you a spirit of fear"
(II Timothy 1:7)

You say: "I'm always worried"
God says: "Cast all your cares on Me"
(I Peter 5:7)

You say: "I feel all alone"
God says: "I will never leave you or forsake you"
(Hebrews 13:5)

Truth with God

Truth of God's Word

Chapter 4: Truth in Relationships

Truth in relationships may be the hardest step of all in the truth process. Sometimes, as discussed, we find it difficult, to be honest with God. But for many, confronting relationships with moms and dads, or brothers and sisters, or ex-spouses and former boy or girlfriends is sometimes harder. We may not find those exchanges to be as loving and gracious as we find God's response to be.

Let's face it, family members and exes can push buttons. It's possible that they may not be as concerned in our freedom as we may be and likely, many of them may not be Christians! But to achieve the freedom and life which one desires, we must be sure that all relationships are mended and healed, or at least, in a healthy process of healing.

There are proper ways to handle the varied relationships which we may find necessary to confront. For instance, I wouldn't suggest meeting, in person, with a former boyfriend or girlfriend with whom you may have had sex when dating, especially if you are now married. A telephone call and letter are even risky ventures, but if communicating with them is necessary to resolve the stronghold which you are confronting, choose the method less likely to stir up old flames. This is the precise situation in which you must hear God! It is why I mentioned, in the first chapter, the principle of *hearing God*, and why I will elaborate on it further in the next chapter. It is absolutely necessary and essential that one has practiced and learned to hear God as opposed to moving forward in the flesh.

In these sensitive situations, ask God to give you a Divine appointment if necessary. You may not even know how to get in touch with the person, so God may need to intervene. It may be that the one offended has passed away so the best way to deal with this is to write them a letter asking them to forgive you, and verbally read it aloud, then burn the letter. Some have even gone to the graveside to ask forgiveness. In every case, the important thing is that your heart be right, and you desire resolution. God knows your heart!

Another important aspect of restoring a relationship is whether the other party is aware of the offense or not. It is not always necessary to approach someone who has no clue that they are remotely involved in your stronghold. Rule of thumb; what is done in secret should be confessed in secret to God, what is done in public should be confessed in public, and what is done between two people should be resolved between the two. The latter scenario might sometimes take a third person, or a "witness" to bring final resolution.

"If your brother sins, go and show him his fault in private; If he listens to you, you have won your brother. But if he does not listen to you, take one or two more with you, so that BY THE MOUTH OF TWO OR THREE WITNESSES EVERY FACT MAY BE CONFIRMED. If he refuses to listen to them, tell it to the church; and if he refuses to listen even to the church, let him be to you as a Gentile and a tax collector." (Matthew 18:15-17)

According to Matthew 18, it is the offended party who initiates the meeting and addresses the offense. The important thing is that the resolution is done humbly, and that much prayer and hearing from God be done before any action is taken. However, don't procrastinate.

When a personal meeting is needed, I suggest you think through the scenario of the offense; whether you or the one you are meeting was the offender, and to what degree of the offense was your part. It has been my experience that in most conflicts, both parties have some percentage of fault. If the offenses can be discussed rationally and without creating a larger problem, then you will naturally move toward deeper healing in that relationship. However, I've seldom seen both parties be able to rehash the details without causing further offenses. Maybe you were 90% the offender and maybe you were only 10% the offender. The point is that you may have offended the other person to some extent.

I want to stress, that it is not essential or even healthy to go back over all the details of the offense. The important point is to just let the person know you were offended and pray that their response will be to ask your forgiveness. Your response is to forgive!

If a congenial resolution can be accomplished, then, by all means, proceed with that method but, if reliving the offenses might cause further damage to the relationship simply take responsibility for your part of the offense and ask forgiveness. You are only responsible for your offense; the other person may not ask forgiveness for their part. Your only responsibility is to make their offense known and to ask forgiveness for any offense on your part.

I believe the wording is very important when restoring broken relationships. If someone comes to you and has been offended, the easy and most common response to them is, "I'm sorry." However, the proper response to them would be, "I'm sorry, will you forgive me?" Hopefully, they will say, "Yes, I forgive you." Being sorry, and asking for forgiveness, are two totally different things. The asking forgiveness part and responding with, "I forgive you" is what will bring healing. The proper response is also very humbling.

If you are going to someone who has offended you, this is the much harder scenario of the two, because you are pointing out their offense. The conversation might sound like this; "Sally, the other day when you said that 'I was a flirt,' that description of me hurt. I want you to know that I love you, and I don't want anything to damage our friendship." At this point in the conversation, you hope that Sally's response would be, "Kaye, I am so sorry, I didn't intend for the comment to hurt you, will you forgive me?" Sally may respond by making excuses and not see it as important, and it may even seem trivial to her. If Sally never sees the importance to ask you to forgive her, then it would be time to involve a third party to resolve the difficulty.

The goal of any broken relationship is always restoration. Restoration is not just mending a disagreement but working to bring the relationship back to its best condition. God is in the business of restoration and His desire is not to just fix the problem, but to restore the relationship to a healthy and fulfilling place.

The fact that we are discussing truth, and the freedom it can bring, accents the importance of freedom in your relationships. Again, this step in the truth process can be the hardest but, it is just as important to take care of your relationships if you desire to experience total freedom. To ignore any step in the truth process, would be like buying a Mercedes and pushing it around everywhere you go. As difficult as restoring relationships can be, it is as important, or even more so, than getting in the Mercedes and driving. Restoring that relationship will not only help you heal but when done properly, it will likely change the life of the other person as well.

When communicating with the offender keep these factors in mind; Remember always to <u>stay in the Spirit</u>, and don't allow anything to move you to the flesh. At least one of you in the conversation needs to always be moving toward God in order to have hope of resolution. Another recommendation is to always be aware of your <u>tone of voice</u> and choice of words as to not further hurt the relationship. Finally, be attentive to <u>listen</u> to the other person's concerns, and open to the fact that YOU might be the problem AND the solution.

Learn to develop every relationship, new and old, with love and truth. Have as a goal; no need to restore any relationship because you have dealt properly, in love, with each person from the beginning.

Truth with God

Truth of God's Word

Truth in Relationship

TRUTH

Chapter 5: Hear the Truth

L earning to *hear the truth* is essential for Christians in all aspects, and facets of our faith.

"My sheep hear My voice, and I know them, and they follow me..." (John 10:27)

"But when He, the Spirit of truth, comes, He will guide you into all the truth; for He will not speak on His own initiative, but whatever He hears, He will speak; and He will disclose to you what is to come." (John 16:13)

Many principles build on one another, much like building blocks. A principle that is vital to the "Truth Principle" Is one of hearing God. It's important for me to spend some time, at this point, explaining hearing God which is foundational to learning the truth.

During my college years and later, as one of the pastors at First Baptist Church, Borger, Texas, I was privileged to meet and learn from some of the best Bible scholars at the time. The church would schedule one or two Bible conferences a year and would invite teachers like Major Ion Thomas who wrote *The Saving Life of Christ*, Manley Beasley author of several writings on *Faith*, Zola Levitt, known for his books on Prophecy including *Coming: The End! Russia & Israel in Prophecy*, and Bill and Anabel Gillham, *A Stillness in the Storm*. I learned and have applied so much from the teaching of these scholars, and I am now teaching, much of what I gleaned from them in those years.

Peter Lord is another scholar who had great Biblical insight and communication skills that impacted my life as well.

It was during one of the Bible conferences that Peter Lord requested volunteers to meet him, separate from the regular conference time. He limited the group to fifteen people and asked that it be young people who were open to a seldom taught principle in the Baptist denomination. My wife, Becky, being very eager to learn, appealed to Peter Lord and asked him if she could join the group even though she wasn't a "young person." Peter agreed and I'm glad he did!

The principle that he taught that afternoon was hearing God. Peter Lord eventually authored a book on the subject, *Hearing God,* published by Baker Book House which I encourage everyone to read. I won't review the hearing God principle, except to say, that Peter Lord challenged those in the class to learn how to listen. He related five questions to the group which he encouraged them to ask God and waited quietly until most of them indicated they had heard an answer to the question.

We make it too difficult; we want to hear an audible voice (which I believe can happen) or see angels, and hear bells and whistles when the most important aspect of hearing God is listening! We live in such a world of distractions which makes it difficult to just *stop* and listen to God.

Becky and I heeded Peter Lord's principle and listened! We listened to the God, who desires more than we will ever realize, to communicate with us. He desires to pull us up close and to reveal to us "the breadth and length and height and depth, and to know the love of Christ which surpasses knowledge." (Ephesians 3:18-19) Just as we all would welcome an audience with one whom we may consider important or famous, the creator of the universe is pursuing an audience with us! Not that we are famous, but we *are* important to Him!

This brings me to the point of this book. God is *not* afraid of, does *not* run from, or *never* pursues anything but the truth. He is the truth!

"I am the way, the truth, and the life..." (John 14:6)

"You will know the truth, and the truth will make you free." (John 8:32)

In fact, when questioned by Pilate at Jesus' trial, Jesus said of Himself, "I have come into the world, to testify to the truth." (John 18:37) Most of us would say that Jesus came into the world to "seek and save that which was lost." (Luke 19:10) He did "seek and save," but it was the *truth* that was his passion and purpose! If Jesus came to "seek and save" the lost but was, in fact, a *lie*, rather than Truth, we would all be deceived! We must all pursue truth, whether physical, mental, or spiritual. To pursue a belief based on conviction is honorable but without truth, it is empty and fruitless.

I once heard an illustration of a man who painted a building. He meticulously cut in around windows and eaves making an effort to do the finest job he could, only to find out that he had put his ladder on the wrong wall. Similarly, we often find ourselves fighting for a cause in which we've "put our ladder on the wrong wall!"

Just as facts and science can sometimes (not always) prove a physical truth, it is more important that we hear God in spiritual truth!

If we would make hearing God as much a priority as we do our other passions, I think we would be amazed at the resourcefulness and productivity of our lives. We would no longer be searching for the "life," but we would be experiencing it! Again, we make it too difficult.

When driving to work, listen! When relaxing or working in the garden, listen! When pillowing your head at night, listen! Having a specific time alone with God is important, but that is *not* the only moment in which God wants to communicate with us! Listen!

God pursues each believer with truth just as He pursues each lost person with truth. He wants everyone to know the truth! We will see as I develop these thoughts on truth, what God's objectives are concerning believers and non-believers.

A group setting is not the ideal situation in which to hear God speak to you. It is much better to ask these questions and others that you might have, in a quiet and uninterrupted time.

When you first listen to a young baby begin to talk, it sometimes takes practice to understand them. I've often noticed mothers interpreting for their young children. The mothers understand them first because they learned to listen and have, obviously, spent more time with the baby!

In the same way, we must learn to listen to God, and understand what His communication is to us. It's not God's difficulty to communicate which is the problem, as much as it is *our* inability, availability, and willingness to listen!

Start with this question to God, "God, how much do you love me?" See what happens! God may bring a scripture to mind, He may place a picture in your thoughts, He may even speak audibly to you. God is not limited in His communication to you, so don't limit your hearing.

Truth with God

Truth of God's Word

Truth in Relationship

Hear the Truth

Chapter 6: Believe the Truth

As difficult as *truth in relationships* can be for most of us, *believing the truth* can be even harder for others. "To have confidence or faith in the truth" is one definition of believing. It sounds fairly simple, but remember, some don't even believe in absolute truth. Another definition of believe would be, "to put your trust in, to adhere to, to stick to like glue." Saying, "I believe," and actually believing, are two different things.

I don't know what more can be done to convince someone of truth, but believing in truth and having confidence in that truth is entirely different. Many have been lied to so often that their confidence is very weak. We have all heard the saying; "seeing is believing." Again, for many, unless they can see something or have scientific proof, it makes it hard to believe. To them, only physical or concrete <u>evidence</u> is convincing. To the skeptics, concerning spiritual truth, I would say, "Check your hearing!" Are you really listening!

"...So, faith comes from hearing, and hearing by the word of Christ." (Romans 10:17)

I was often asked to preach on Sunday mornings during my Student Ministry days, so one particular Sunday I chose the subject of Faith. I asked a young freshman boy to come to the stage and assist me in an illustration. The stage was probably three or four feet off the ground, so I asked the young man to go to the edge, turn his back to the audience, and free-fall backward toward the ground. Of course, he laughed, and then I said, "Wait, close your eyes, and put your arms to your side. Now, without looking, call six people whom you trust, one at a time to stand behind you." He started with his dad, then our Youth intern and on until six men stood behind him. Then he asked each man individually, starting with his dad, "Dad, are you there?" He replied, "yes, and I will catch you." And on in that order, he asked each man the same question. Then I said, "Dillon, did you hear the men behind you?" "Yes," he replied. "Do you trust them to catch you?" I asked. "They better!" he shouted. Then Dillon, on my command, fell straight backward, and the men succeeded in catching him safely.

This illustrates the passage, "faith comes from hearing" very well. Dillon did not see the men behind him; he only heard them and trusted them to catch him. Believing the truth first comes from hearing the truth. We must have confidence in that truth.

Believing the truth not only comes from hearing it, but we must know the truth. We should be students of the truth, so much so, that as lies come, we can reference the truth at a moment's notice. That is why memorizing truth is so important as well. I am amazed at the number of "born again Christians" who do not know the Bible or take the time to memorize it for themselves. Sadly, many are Biblically illiterate!

When I was in college I would assist a building contractor on available weekends and during summer months. I discovered that most cities have varying city codes. Even though cities in one region may have nearly identical building codes, they might differ in limited practices.

The contractor and I were asked to finish a job on which another contractor had broken codes. The other contractor used concrete depths and reinforcement codes for the city in which he lived, but was only thirty miles away from the building site. Unfortunately for him, the codes were slightly different in the neighboring city. Not studying and knowing the codes was a terminal move for the previous builder, which resulted in him losing the contract.

Christians need to know the truth! We need to memorize, study, and hear God's Word, which helps shape an understanding and relationship with the author, God. It is hard to believe something or someone in whom there is no relationship. Just as a builder needs to study and know building codes, it is just as important for Christians to know and study the Bible.

I recently had a man knock on my door wanting help with gas and food. He explained to me that he was an evangelist and had just spent his last dollar to repair his fuel pump. In the process of the visit, he delighted in telling me that he had memorized the entire Bible. He also related that he had been married 3 times and had recently been released from prison. My conclusion was that even though one may know the truth, and in this case memorized it, observing the truth is much more important than just knowing it.

As children, we have all had scary times, but knowing that our mother or father was there, would help us make it through. It was because we knew our folks loved us and would never want to harm us. To go through a scary time with someone we don't know is hard. We can believe more easily in someone when trust has been established. In the same way, we can begin to believe the truth when our relationship with the source of that truth is developed.

Each of us needs to build trust of everyone, with whom we are asked to be dependent.

As a young boy, I remember hearing the story of Charles Blondin, the famous French tightrope walker. He attempted, in June of 1859, to become the first person to walk a tightrope that extended more than a quarter of a mile across Niagara Falls. Blondin made the trip across at over 150 feet above the falls, several times to the amazement and excitement of the large crowd gathered on each end of the rope. He crossed each time with a different courageous feat; riding a bicycle, carrying a stove, and at one point, Blondin walked blindfolded pushing a wheelbarrow across. Finally, Blondin asked the crowd if they thought he could walk the wheelbarrow across with a person riding inside. With rousing applause, everyone cheered, and all agreed that he could, to which he responded, "Do I have any volunteers to get in?"

Truth, and our confidence in that truth, is only as fruitful as our willingness to "get in." No one took Blondin up on his offer to walk a person across in the wheelbarrow that day but, later in August of 1859, his manager, Harry Colcord, did ride across the falls on Blondin's back. We might all agree, in that instance, that Harry Colcord was crazy, but we can't argue that he didn't have faith.

As uncertain as the truth might seem to us, sometimes we must "get in," and we must believe. Spiritual truth does not always make sense to us, but we must put our trust in the author of our faith. As we learn the truth, and as the truth begins to set us free, then believing the truth becomes a part of us and we are no longer deceived with the lie.

Lie: "You can't do anything right!" Truth: "I can do all things through Christ who strengthens me." (Philippians 4:13)

We live in a generation where children and young people are being told they are worthless, that they will never succeed, that they are too large or too poor, even too stupid to learn. All these lies are exposing our future. It is important that we as parents, teachers, pastors, coaches, or anyone who may influence these young lives speak truth to them. We need to encourage and love them, and help them to believe the truth. We ourselves must believe the truth before we can show anyone else the truth.

Believing is to put your trust in, to adhere to, to stick to like glue. We need to "get in." It is one thing to believe that there *is* a God; it's entirely another thing to believe *in* God!

I know believing is hard; it is hard to believe a doctor when he tells you, "the surgery is a simple procedure." We all want to believe that, but we always seem to lose a little sleep the night before, don't we? For some, boarding an airplane brings a little anxiety even though we know that 99.9% of all flights make their destination safely, maybe not uneventfully, but safely. Unless we've done something routinely for a long time, there will always be a little apprehension, and to be honest, a routine can become pride if we aren't careful.

God knew our tendency toward fear, doubt, and lack of faith when He said to the disciples, "Because of the littleness of your faith; for truly I say to you, if you have faith the size of a mustard seed, you will say to this mountain, 'Move from here to there,' and it will move; and nothing will be impossible to you. "…But this kind does not go out except by prayer and fasting." (Matthew 17:20-21)

God is not asking us to have enormous faith, but only that of a mustard seed size, and that comes by prayer and fasting. Again, it goes back to *knowing* the source of the truth. Our relationship with God *cannot* be a casual acquaintance or just a moment of reflection when we happen to think about it. Faith is developed, nurtured, and cemented in us when we truly know God! When we *know* God, we believe Him!

We cannot simply know the truth, but we must believe it, and know that it is Satan who continues to promote the lie which consumes and devours our soul if we allow it.

Truth with God

Truth of God's Word

Truth in Relationships

Hear the Truth

Believe the Truth

   (know and memorize the truth)

TRUTH

Chapter 7: Live the Truth

Have you ever known someone to espouse a belief yet lives the opposite of that belief? I think we all have, so that's why we need to *Live the Truth!* Don't choose to live any longer in the bondage of a lie, especially knowing that Christ came to set us free!

For many Christians, we have lived our lives day in and day out with "business as usual." We don't really expect to see God do anything in our lives or even consider that He really desires to. After all, who am I? I am not David who slew a giant as a teenage boy and later became king! I am not Paul who visually saw the Lord on the road to Damascus, and eventually penned much of the New Testament! Who am I?

There we go, believing the lie again! Let me show you who you really are, or better yet, let the Word of God show you who you are in Christ.

[16] "that He would grant <u>you</u>, according to the riches of His glory, to be strengthened <u>with power</u> through His Spirit in the inner man, [17] so that Christ may dwell in <u>your</u> hearts through faith; and that <u>you</u>, being rooted and grounded in love, [18] may be able to comprehend with all the saints what is the breadth and length and height and depth, [19] and to know the love of Christ which surpasses knowledge, <u>that you may be filled up to all the fullness of God.</u>

[20] <u>Now to Him who is able to do far more abundantly beyond all that we ask or think</u>, according to the power that works <u>within us</u>, [21] to Him be the glory in the church and in Christ Jesus to all generations forever and ever. Amen." (Ephesians 3:16-21)

[37] "But in all these things <u>we overwhelmingly conquer</u> through Him who loved us. [38] For I am convinced that neither death, nor life, nor angels, nor principalities, nor things present, nor things to come, nor powers, [39] nor height, nor depth, nor any other created thing, will be able to separate us from the love of God, which is in Christ Jesus our Lord." (Romans 8:37-39)

"Truly, truly, I say to you, <u>he who believes in Me, the *works* that I do, he will do also</u>; and <u>greater works</u> than these <u>he</u> will do; because I go to the Father.[13] Whatever <u>you</u> ask

86

in My name, that will I do, so that the Father may be glorified in the Son. [14] If you ask Me anything in My name, I will do *it*. [15] "If you love Me, you will keep My commandments." (John 14:12-15)

God's word is clear, and I believe it demonstrates that most Christians are accomplishing far less than God ever wanted us to accomplish! We have all heard incredible stories of God working in Christians around the world but why is God not working like that in us?

My experience with a man on an airplane to Pittsburg, which I will reference now, but will explain later in detail in chapter 12, is a perfect example of what happens when we begin to *live the Truth*. I don't believe for one second that the man behind me *just happened* to be there at that time, and *just happened* to have a *Survival Kit*. Nor do I believe that the businessman on the other side of the flight attendant *just happened* to have a desire to receive what I was sharing with the lady. I could fill this book with illustrations of Divine appointments just since learning this principle! I wonder sometimes, how many Divine appointments I may have missed, in the past, simply because I was not available to God, or *living the truth!*

We all know what we can do in the flesh because we've been doing it for so long, but what can we do in the Spirit? All the great men and women in the Bible faced difficult circumstances, and maybe more difficult than any of us will ever face. If we study their lives, we can see that, just like us, their dependency on the Lord was the key to their miraculous journeys.

Living the truth comes from the confidence we have *in* the truth! It is the truth that is our confidence, not our flesh or anything we can do. This may be the case in spiritual or physical truth.

A local businessman and church member, whom I consider a friend, thought our church, for some reason, spent way too much money on mission trips. He made that observation many times in finance committee meetings which I attended, and in conversations with many of the mission team members, but never personally to me. One day as we passed in the hall, he took the opportunity to express his concern for what he thought was extravagant monies the church was spending on, in his words, "a vacation, financed by the church." We had a quick conversation about it, but both determined that the discussion needed to include the pastor as well.

When we met with the pastor, the gentleman began laying out his argument for why the church was spending too much money on missions. The hall discussions had changed from only mission trips to now including missions in general. Missions was a budgeted item; mission trips were not.

I am not a confrontational person. My Motivational gift is mercy, so to confront someone, goes against all that I am. However, since learning the *Truth Principle* years before, I knew that I not only needed to *Live the Truth*, which is our discussion in this section of the book, but I also needed to *Speak the Truth*, which we will cover more in the next section.

When one knows the truth, that truth will bring freedom, boldness, and confidence to live it out! After about twenty minutes of the gentleman's critique of the subject, I asked if I could inject my thoughts. I pointed out to the gentleman that, "most of the trips were paid for by the individuals themselves, either with personal funds or with a love offering given voluntarily by people who wanted to help the teams go on the trips. Usually, the love offering covered less than half of an individual's way. The leader's way is paid out of a love offering which was agreed on in guidelines set by the Mission's Committee and voted on by the church. The trips are very taxing and hard work for each team member that goes. It has been described accordingly by many of the team members in testimony times at the end of the trips." I continued, "Very little if any funds come from budgeted money unless we take into consideration some postage and other minor office supplies. So please tell me, how is the church paying for anyone's way other than the offering money that is given freely?" After a few seconds of silence, he replied, "I think the teams are taking advantage of those giving the love offering!" I asked, "Do the people give voluntarily, or do we force them to give?" He chuckled, and then I asked him, "Have you ever given to the mission trip offering?" With that, the discussion ended fairly quickly. I told him that we did not agree, but I still loved him as a brother. It is hard to argue with the truth.

It is not enough to just know the truth or believe the truth, but we must begin to *live the truth!* Sometimes living the truth will involve confrontation but our confidence is that of knowing the truth and living it out. Most of the time, living the truth will be acting on God's direction and voice, and watching Him do things that can only be explained by Him! That's the fun part. Other times it will involve confrontation. Love must be the motivation of any confrontation and the restoration of the relationship.

After the first five or six years of going to China, our teams had built many close and meaningful relationships. One of those relationships was with a young lady named Ai-Tow-Mei whom we had met in a local business. Although her business moved location almost every year that we returned, we somehow found her. In the sixth and seventh year, however, we were unable to find Ai-Tow-Mei and reasoned that she had either left the city or maybe because its population of 400,000 would make it like finding a needle in a haystack. In the third year of not seeing Ai-Tow-Mei, I shared with my team that the Lord had told me we would see Divine appointments that year. One day while coming out of a sporting goods store, where we bought soccer balls for the kids, I heard a female voice shout, "Awndy!" It was Ai-Tow-Mei! Living the truth will open doors that no man can close, and lead to appointments that only God can arrange.

Stop believing the lie that God can't use you in incredible ways like He did David or Paul...He can! The awesome thing is that He wants to! We need to live every day with the confidence of the truth and not with the lie Satan wants us to believe.

"The thief comes only to steal and kill and destroy; I (Jesus) came that they may have life, and have it abundantly." (John 10:10)

Like David, Like Paul, and like Ruth, we all have a story that God wants to write. God desires to use us in such a way that we are a living Bible. We must live God's story that He wants to write through us. God's story is only written when we die to our fleshly desires, hear God, and obey His direction for our lives. Ask God to author your story and then, let Him fulfill it!

A well-known illustration of the three circles; Lost, Carnal, and Spirit-filled, put the carnal man on the throne and God off the throne. However, the reality is that God NEVER leaves the throne, it's just that carnal man refuses to bow to the king! We must die to our flesh and bow (surrender) to God, allowing Him to direct our paths!

Ordinary people do extraordinary things when they let an extraordinary God write their otherwise ordinary story! *Live* the truth!

In the Second and Third chapters of John, three other aspects of Truth are discussed which, I think, fall under *Living the Truth*.

Love in Truth

Love in Truth, discussed in 2 John 1:1-3 is a concept mostly lost in recent years. It seems that many relationships are built on what one can gain from the other person, rather than what one can give! This is especially true in middle school and high school relationships, but it is more common in adults nowadays, and it's just that adults are better at disguising it!

Relationships that *love in truth* include honesty, giving, integrity, vulnerability, and forgiveness. These relationships are those that last and are sustainable through a lifetime. Marriage is designed by God to be this kind of relationship, but many marriages today are based on the "middle school" principle of "what can I get" and that leads to the ominous divorce rate that we see today.

Love in Truth relationships can and should be developed with peers and family as well. I am blessed to have many *Love in Truth* relationships with some brothers in Christ, but especially with one man in particular, who is closer than a brother and knows everything about me. I know of men who served together on the battlefield and talk often of the sacrificial love they had for one another.

These relationships can be developed with couples as well. A married couple needs to have other couples in their lives who have a bond of love, in which honesty, giving, integrity, vulnerability, and forgiveness exemplifies their friendship.

Love in Truth is a lost art and is seriously lacking in our world today.

As I write, my incredible wife Becky is loving in truth. She sits with my mom (94 years old) who is dying of a painful, debilitating form of cancer. She feeds her and helps her to the bathroom. She applies medicine to the wound and cleans the blood that occasionally forms. We have no sisters in my family, only my two brothers and me. Becky has become a living Ruth, loving her mother-in-law like her own mother. Becky is a testimony to my Mom and me of *Loving in truth!*

Walk in Truth

Another aspect of truth mentioned in 3 John 1:3-4 is that of Walking in Truth. We can know the truth, believe the truth, hear the truth, but Walking in the Truth is a harder task. It's much like weight loss; we can read about diets and exercise, we can discuss it with our friends, and even buy weight loss equipment, but actually doing what it takes to lose the weight is harder. Walking in truth is living the life out in public and abiding in the Spirit when the flesh wants to pull you away. That must be the battle my wife is experiencing in caring for my mom.

It is easy to react to circumstances around us, with the flesh, if we are not consciously trusting the Holy Spirit within to guide us in our reactions to the world.

The same is true with *walking in truth*, it requires of us applying what we know, and then to hear and believe.

Workers of Truth

Also, in 3 John 1:8, the author discusses *Workers of Truth*. I think walking and working seem similar, they both imply action, but walking in the truth is more a mindset, workers of truth are carrying out the plan. It is doing, with action, what we believe, know, and hear. It is the worker of truth who is promised a blessing. If we are not walking in truth and maintaining that mindset, working in truth will never happen.

"But prove yourselves doers of the word, and not merely hearers who delude themselves. For if anyone is a hearer of the word and not a doer, he is like a man who looks at his natural face in a mirror; for once he has looked at himself and gone away, he has immediately forgotten what kind of person he was. But one who looks intently at the perfect law, the law of liberty, and abides by it, not having become a forgetful hearer but an effectual doer, this man will be blessed in what he does." (James 1:22-25)

Live the Truth

Living the truth encompasses our loving, walking, and working truth! Truth must be our life!

Truth with God

Truth of God's Word

Truth in Relationship

Hear the Truth

Believe the Truth

  (know and memorize the truth)

Live the Truth

  (Love in Truth, Walk in Truth, Workers of Truth)

Chapter 8: Speak the Truth

To *Speak the Truth* indicates action! This is the part of the *Truth Principle* where we have the privilege to minister to others. Speaking truth can bring healing, freedom, and restoration. That's why it is so important that when the truth is learned, we need to practice communicating it as well.

Speaking the truth can sometimes run into walls, and that is to be expected, but believe me; Satan does not want truth spoken! Knowing truth does not excite Satan either, but he certainly doesn't want us sharing and speaking it to others. Satan does know the truth!

"Then the devil took him into the holy city and had him stand on the pinnacle of the temple, and said to Him 'If you are the Son of God, throw Yourself down; For it is written,

'HE WILL COMMAND HIS ANGELS CONCERNING YOU'; and 'ON *their* HANDS THEY WILL BEAR YOU UP, SO THAT YOU WILL NOT STRIKE YOUR FOOT AGAINST A STONE.'" (Matthew 4:5-6)

With the revelation of truth comes responsibility. Some can interpret our speaking of truth as pride or ego, and it can sometimes appear that way. Consequently, we need to avoid speaking in the flesh rather than the Spirit. Again, *hearing God* is important, and we must always speak with humility and love to one another, it doesn't mean, however, that we shouldn't speak boldly.

Speaking Truth to Others

Speaking truth to others is one important aspect of speaking truth. Sometimes it may be speaking the truth in passing or in <u>conversation,</u> and sometimes it may be speaking the truth in <u>confrontation.</u>

I have a very dear seventy-eight-year-old friend who loves God with all his heart and would never want to misrepresent God in any way. In worship, he is very demonstrative and when anyone preaches, "Amens" are very common. He is naturally an encourager to everyone.

On a road trip with a group of guys one day, the subject of "life" in worship services was being discussed. He mentioned that too many Christians just observed worship rather than involving themselves with worship. In the process of the conversation, I asked the group, "Do you think 'Amen' is always a proper response to comments made during sermons?" He said, "You bet!" That very day the pastor had said, "Even the best Christians sometimes sin." To which this gentleman responded, "Amen!" I explained that "The word Amen means 'so be it.'" When he realized the contradiction, the gentleman's little impish grin that he sometimes has, came across his face and he began to chuckle about his response to that statement. This had been a friendly and somewhat playful conversation among four or five friends, but just two weeks later he caught me in the hall at church and said that the discussion made him think about what he was agreeing with, in his response of "Amen." He said, "I began to be more careful, with what I said 'Amen' to!" Thankfully, it didn't diminish his demonstration of worship, but it did motivate him to be more attentive with his responses.

There are some people in our lives, who are very approachable and with whom it is very easy, to be honest. That was true with the seventy-eight-year-old friend I mentioned above. Along with four or five other men, we have ministered together in many prisons, from Chicago to Florida for over twenty years. Our conversations are always amusing and playful with occasional seriousness thrown in for fun.

It is not always that easy to speak the truth, and not everyone is approachable. In fact, certain times necessitate speaking the truth when we would just as soon have a root canal!

As mentioned earlier, our families can sometimes be the hardest to confront. Our workplace can also be a difficult setting to discuss truth. Some of the reasons for difficulty include proximity; you spend a lot of time with them, at work for instance, and there is nowhere else to go if things go south. Another difficulty would be because you simply have more to lose, especially with family. No one wants to lose a job or a friend, but family is for life, and there is so much more invested. Even with these negatives to consider, truth is always the best direction to go. The proverbial "elephant in the room" is always better when dealt with, than ignored; and the sooner the better, because there is much less mess to clean up!

One solution to less confrontation is to learn to set up healthy boundaries in our lives or we will find ourselves controlled by others. I am a people person, and I enjoy all the conversations of which I am a part. Not using personal time wisely can be a negative aspect when engaging in too much conversation. Sometimes I have all day to talk, and other times I have other important projects that need to be accomplished. I have learned that when my time is limited, to let those who may need to visit with me know that I have a meeting, or a project scheduled and that I may have only a few minutes to visit. There are always kind and gracious ways to guard your time.

When all my eleven grandchildren lived close, it was important for my wife and me to set boundaries or we would be spending all our weekends and free time with childcare. We always enjoyed our time with the grandkids, and we miss all of them not being near but, it was important as well, that attention be given to my marriage and our relationship as a couple.

In both cases, the truth needed to be spoken in love and boundaries set. When one is open and honest, and able to set boundaries, it will help avoid some of the pitfalls and misunderstandings that can occur without them.

Another important word, when spoken in love, is "no." This was especially hard for me to learn because of my motivational gift of mercy. It seemed that all my time was full, and I seldom had time for myself or my family. I never wanted to disappoint anyone, so I wouldn't say no. I eventually learned to have a calendar and to let the calendar be my friend. To this day I don't carry a calendar with me, but my main calendar is at the office. When anyone asks me about a particular date, and if I'm available, I will say, "I need to check my calendar."

A pastor friend, Dan Yeary, taught The Metro Youth Ministers, several years ago, to be sure to sit down with their family, and schedule important dates at the first of the year, or as soon as family dates are known. When a good calendar is maintained, it helps one to say, "no" when you need to, and the important family and personal dates should already be in place.

Speaking the Truth in Confrontation

When speaking the truth in confrontation is necessary, it is mandatory that one hears God, and that he checks his heart for the proper motivation. Confrontation should never be done to prove one's point or just to expose the fault, but only to reveal the truth, and to restore relationships.

I remember a church that announced through their leadership that one of the organization's employees was leaving and, in their announcement, inferred that the employee was taking another job. When the former employee remained in the city several months afterward, the congregation knew that something was not right. The week of the announcement, another employee and I found a letter left in the office copy machine, which instructed the former employee that he was to resign, and not talk about it with anyone, or his severance would be stopped. This was a situation in which I knew the truth had to be exposed for the unity of the church, and that I had to confront the leadership and reveal their lie. I never disclosed to the leadership that I even had the letter because I wanted them to admit to the truth willingly. I'm sorry to say that the leadership denied what I knew to be true, and that organization has continued to suffer because of it. I did what God instructed me to do, unfortunately, without ever seeing a complete resolution. To their credit, several of the leadership asked me privately to forgive them which, of course, I did.

Confrontation is never pleasant but usually necessary. Don't forget to pray and hear God's wisdom before entering this unpredictable arena of truth.

Speaking Truth Against Strongholds

Speaking truth against strongholds was touched on earlier when we discussed the *truth of God's word* in chapter three. This is especially important because it is only, truth and the power of Christ's shed blood that can have any effect on the power of Satan and his strongholds in our lives.

It is important when dealing personally with strongholds whether anger, lust, gossip, or any of the many lies Satan throws at us, to do so with truth. As you begin to see victory in the area of strongholds in your own life, I encourage you to be sensitive to those around you who might need to learn the *truth principle* in dealing with their own strongholds. Of course, we don't want to go around looking for those folks but learn to be sensitive to those whom God might be putting in your life who may actually need your help.

Learning to speak the truth, automatically sets needed boundaries, and will eventually bring the freedom that would have otherwise never been experienced.

Truth with God

Truth of God's Word

Truth in Relationship

Hear the Truth

Believe the Truth

   (know and memorize the truth)

Live the Truth

   (Love in Truth, Walk in Truth, Workers of Truth)

Speak the Truth

   (To Others, In Confrontation, Against Strongholds)

TRUTH

Chapter 9: Pray the Truth

Praying the Truth is a very powerful part of the truth principle! If the word of God is effective against demonic strongholds, then it is just as effective when praying. For many, prayer has never developed past; "thank you for our food and the hands that have prepared it, forgive us of our sins and those who have sinned against us." They pray just as they have seen others pray but have never been taught the power of prayer!

"For the word of God is living and active and sharper than any two-edged sword, and piercing as far as the division of soul and spirit, of both joints and marrow, and able to judge the thoughts and intentions of the heart." (Hebrews 4:12)

God wants to hear our hearts when we pray and that is important, especially, when we first meet Him in the day. Our prayers, however, should not remain just on a request level, but can and should move to a deeper conversation with God. It is important when interceding on behalf of someone, or for personal needs, that we pray truth!

Scripture is a very powerful weapon when spoken in prayer. When we pray scripture, we are praying in the authority of God's word! If healing is needed, pray scriptures that include God's promises about healing. If you are imploring God on behalf of a lost or rebellious person, use salvation scriptures as your authority for that request. If strongholds of fear, or anger, or depression are at war within you or for someone with whom you are interceding, apply scriptures that relate to those strongholds and claim authority by the word of God!

It is very important that Christians learn and memorize scripture as a weapon against sin!

"Your word I have treasured in my heart, that I may not sin against You." (Psalm 119:11)

The memorized word of God helps us to keep sin at bay in our lives. Satan hates God's word and it acts as a guard at the door of our minds. While praying scripture will act as the authority we need, it is not a substitute for the Holy Spirit. If we would be honest with ourselves, I think we would see that many of our prayers are no more than flesh, and the results are no more than what flesh can accomplish. As Christians, we have the Holy Spirit living within us, but too often we operate only in the flesh. We must learn to move from the Outer Court, through the Holy Place, to the Holy of Holies where the Spirit of God resides and pray, not in the flesh, but in the Spirit of God!

What keeps the "average" Christian from moving into the presence of God, and communicating to Him, with compassion? splangkh-nid'-zom-ahee.

"Seeing the people, He felt compassion for them because they were distressed and dispirited like sheep without a shepherd." (Matthew 9:36)

The Greek word for compassion, splangkh-nid'-zom-ahee, means He was moved within His Bowels! Jesus was moved to physical agony when He prayed, something few Christians ever experience. The reason few Christians experience this kind of prayer is because of sin; we are afraid of what will happen if we pray with passion, and we are concerned with what people will think when we pray passionately. The only excuse we have for not meeting God with passion is sin! We can make all the excuses we want, but it really comes down to sin.

To actually pray the truth, it needs to be done in the Spirit, not the flesh, and by the authority of the word of God. This kind of prayer is that of miracles. This kind of prayer is that of which Jesus spoke in John 14.

"Truly, truly, I say to you, he who believes in Me, the works that I do, he will do also; and greater works than these he will do; because I go to the Father. Whatever you ask in My name, that will I do, so that the Father may be glorified in the Son. If you ask Me anything in My name, I will do it." (John 14:12-15)

It is difficult to achieve a passionate moving prayer in a public setting, not that it can't and doesn't happen, it can and does happen. I remember on many occasions being part of large and small prayer groups where the Holy Spirit moved, and God accomplished more than we ever expected or could explain.

It's not often in public prayer, however, that the heart of God moves on my heart in such a way to embolden me to the truth. It's my personal intimate time with God that brings the confidence to live life the way God intended us to live it; truthfully, confidentially, boldly, and outwardly to a world that needs to see that truth. Our prayer closet becomes a foxhole where the only thing that matters is LIFE! It is then, that we are not concerned with what others think or hear, or eloquent discourse, but with the war around us and the defeat of the enemy! When the "Church" learns to battle in prayer over things that matter to God then, prayer will matter to the church!

It is the prayer of a righteous man that will see God move!

Truth with God

Truth of God's Word

Truth in Relationship

Hear the Truth

Believe the Truth

> *(know and memorize the truth)*

Live the Truth

> *(Love in Truth, Walk in Truth, Workers of Truth)*

Speak the Truth

> *(To Others, In Confrontation, Against Strongholds)*

Pray the Truth

Chapter 10: Proclaim the Truth

I mentioned in an earlier chapter that I think any belief that can't stand up to debate or intellectual discussion is probably a flawed and weak belief at best. Truth should *never* be afraid to be tested because the truth will always stand the test!

We should never be afraid to discuss the truth. In fact, I believe truth; when practiced on every level of life, as we have touched on in this book, would result in a changed world!

For too long, the politically correct world has tried to silence truth while promoting their personal beliefs as truth.

"The world will not be destroyed by those who do evil, but by those who watch them without doing anything."
–Albert Einstein 1953

"All that is necessary for the triumph of evil is that good men do nothing." –Edmund Burke 1770

Banging his shoe on the table in 1956, I remember Russian Secretary, Nikita Khrushchev declared, "We will take America without firing a shot...we will bury you! We shall destroy you from within."

Mar 28, 2015, standyourground.com statistics:

[Comparing the culture of the '50s to that of 1998] violent criminal offenses have exploded upward by 700%. Premarital sex among 18-year-olds has jumped from 30% of the population to 70%. Tax rates for a family of four have skyrocketed 500%, consuming a fourth of their income. Divorce rates have quadrupled. Illegitimate births among Black Americans have soared from approximately 23% to more than 68%. Illegitimacy itself has jumped from a nationwide total of 5% to nearly 30% nationwide - a rise of 600%. Cases of sexually transmitted diseases have risen by 150%. Teenage pregnancies are up by several thousand percent and teen suicides have risen by 200%. Between 1950 and 1979 - serious crime committed by children under 15 has risen by 11,000%.

The statistics prove America's internal demise, and without a voice of truth, the downhill slide will continue. More than ever, those who know, and practice truth need to stand up and proclaim it!

The opposition has "heavy hitters" and has been systematic, organized, and determined for many years. The battle is not against "flesh and blood," but it is Satan who comes to "steal, kill and destroy!" No matter how big the resistance, "good men" and women need to stand up and be heard. Those who oppose truth do not have truth at their disposal, so they must lie, malign, and degrade those who do. For Christians, the battle is not ours, but the Lord's. We are to "speak the truth, in love," BUT, WE ARE TO SPEAK THE TRUTH!

"But in all things, we overwhelmingly conquer through Him who loved us." (Romans 8:37)

We need to learn to always speak the truth. Not only should we speak the truth, but we need to be proclaimers of truth, and there is a difference.

Broadcast is another synonym for proclaim. The adverb broadcast indicates to reach the most amount of people possible. Secular Humanist's began with a strategy to condense the number of people they wanted to reach, and then reached them with every means possible! They have used education, politics, television programs, moral issues, rights, environment, population, and books to name a few of their techniques to "broadcast" their message!

We can begin "broadcasting" by finally ceasing to be silent about the truth, and search for other ways that we can make a difference.

First, seek truth in your own life and ask God to heal your areas of "strongholds" as we covered in chapter five: *The Truth of God's Word.* Know that you can be confident in the truth and depend on God to strengthen you in your doubt and weakness.

"And He has said to me, 'My grace is sufficient for you, for power is perfected in weakness. Most gladly, therefore, I will rather boast about my weaknesses, so that the power of Christ may dwell in me. Therefore, I am well content with weaknesses, with insults, with distresses, with persecutions, with difficulties, for Christ's sake; for when I am weak, then I am strong.'" (2 Corinthians 12:9, 10)

Write letters, make phone calls, and send emails to your congressmen and senators regularly! We should also let The President know of our feelings and speak the truth on issues that may damage our country.

Be involved in your school and civic organizations such as the school board and city council. One does not have to be on the school board or city council, but simply needs to attend meetings and send letters. Let your concerns be known! Organize those who share your concerns and challenge them to be involved as well. Many adverse decisions are made merely because there is no opposition.

Be active in your school; read what your children read, ask questions about what they learned today, and monitor their computer use, including homework. An alarming trend has taken place over the last few years. Schools have been encouraging students to do more of their work at school. The reason given has been to preserve the books and textbooks, but the true reason is to hide what is being taught to your students in those books. With online assignments, it has become more convenient to give homework yet conceal the content from parents. Don't doubt me if you have not investigated this fact!

Not only should parents be active in the school and civic organizations, but they should also be informing and instructing their kids of the efforts that are taking place so that they can be alert to destructive teaching and agendas. I would caution parents to use discretion and avoid stirring up fear and anxiety in their kids. Avoid creating extremism and looking for danger at every turn but help them to be wise and attentive.

Be active in any organized attempt to make your voice heard. Don't be passive any longer. Radical groups are very open and demonstrative in their beliefs and their broadcasting of those beliefs. Don't depend on just your "vote" and prayers for the defense of evil but be doers! Many illustrations of God calling on men to act out their faith and the battle for truth fill the scriptures. American's have gotten comfortable in their belief that the right thing will be done, but that may no longer be true, and should no longer be taken for granted.

"But prove yourselves doers of the word, and not merely hearers who delude themselves." (James 1:22)

Be informed! Take time to listen, read and study the facts, and know what you believe. Better yet, don't just take your values and standards for granted, know why you believe what you believe! Your first resource needs to be the Word of God! Know, memorize, study, and use the Word as your standard of Truth! Anything that opposes God's Word is not the truth, so it is imperative to know His Word!

If no one in your area or city is active in the solutions I have suggested, then you need to step up and organize a plan of action. Yes, it is hard work, and opposition will come. We are talking about the systematic destruction of America, your family, and your freedom. We must be active, organized, informed, and prayed up.

The world has been very methodical and deliberate in its attempt to influence and change society. Unlike the Church, they have slowly and successfully made changes and modifications in education, entertainment, families, politics, and now even the Church, while the Church has developed a more "come and hear" attitude rather than a "go and make a difference" approach. The Church is in desperate need to look beyond their own traditional, and sometimes judgmental, walls and develop a vision to reach "out" to their communities and beyond. We need to have a plan and strategy to make a difference in every area of our world and begin to reclaim what we have allowed the world to steal.

While I believe a large-scale movement and organizational plan is needed, it must start with individual churches making a difference where they are. Churches must get out of the box and begin developing a vision for their communities. We must give extravagantly, love unconditionally, pray passionately, and go indefinitely. Churches can no longer just pray, and hope things will change, but the Church needs to become the difference makers in our world! We are not just teachers, pastors, and workers, we are LIFE changers!

Finally, the Word of God, more than any one document, has been opposed, maligned, and fought. It has been burned and destroyed worldwide yet it remains. Jesus, the central character, though innocent, as proven by law and proclaimed by Pilot, was sought to be killed in an attempt to silence the Truth! Even His death was not enough to silence Him or His purpose. With all the history of violence and opposition against God and His Word, no one or nothing has been able to disprove even one thing about Jesus, the Word of God, and their claims. In fact, since from Bible times to the present, more proof is continually discovered from excavations to other findings on many fronts.

The world events, as an example, especially Middle Eastern conflicts and developments there, are occurring just as written about in books of the Bible like Daniel, Matthew, and Revelation.

To those who doubt the truth about God, Jesus, and the Bible; show me any single evidence of proof against them. It is not there, and it will never be found. Please consider God, Jesus, and the Bible as truth and find that for which so many are searching. God hates your sin, not you! He loved you so much that He willingly gave His life, so that you might find life, and find it abundantly! "The truth will set you free!"

Truth with God

Truth of God's Word

Truth in Relationship

Hear the Truth

Believe the Truth

   (know and memorize the truth)

Live the Truth

   (Love in Truth, Walk in Truth, Workers of Truth)

Speak the Truth

   (To Others, In Confrontation, Against Strongholds)

Pray the Truth

Proclaim the Truth

TRUTH

Chapter 11: Desire the Truth

None of the principles of truth are achievable unless we first *Desire the Truth*. Hearing, believing, praying, and knowing the truth are needed and are good, but we must develop a desire and a hunger for the truth before it will be accomplished in our lives!

Not only is the desire for truth lacking in our churches, but it originates in us; the people who comprise the Church. To pursue truth is exhausting, especially if we attempt it in the flesh. We must know that the truth will eventually bring freedom. It will bring emotional and spiritual healing that will replace the exhaustion with joy and fulfillment.

We allow ourselves to develop desires for food, sports, and clothing, along with so many other things, but a desire for truth and the realization of it will bring more satisfaction and "completion" than any other pursuit!

Adrian Rogers once related an illustration that gives a good picture of the need to desire truth. When one is born, we are <u>fed</u> until we learn to <u>feed ourselves</u> then, we should eventually <u>feed others</u>.

Desiring truth is moving from just being fed, like babies, to feeding ourselves spiritually, and eventually feeding others as well. When a child never learns to feed himself, it's considered abnormal. However, when a "Christian" never grows past being fed, we make excuses such as being too busy, or not understanding the Bible, etc. It's abnormal!

For the Christian, there is no excuse but laziness for the ignorance of God's word! If we have a true desire to know God, we will be hearing, knowing, and praying like never before.

The greatest need in our world today is that of the desire for truth, and the exercise of it in our homes, churches, and leadership. Truth is discouraged, dishonored, manipulated, and abused for political and personal gain, and has been so distorted that the current generation does not even recognize the truth.

Therefore, we need to desire truth more than ever in our lives and begin to live it out as a witness to our children and grandchildren. Without that desire and demonstration of truth, a "lie will become truth, and truth will become a lie"

We will discuss the deliberate demise of our world, and that of Christianity in the next few chapters, but the blame lies solely on Christians and their reluctance to desire the truth!

"(If) My people who are called by My name humble themselves and pray and seek My face and turn from their wicked ways, then I will hear from heaven, will forgive their sin and will heal their land." (2 Chronicles 7:14)

We must be "doers of the word, and not hearers only!" James 1:22 (KJV)

Ask God to give you a *desire for truth*, and a desire to be truthful with God, know the truth of God's Word, develop truth in relationships, hear the truth, believe the truth, live the truth, love in truth, walk in truth, be workers of truth, speak the truth, pray the truth, and proclaim the truth!

Truth with God

Truth of God's Word

Truth in Relationship

Hear the Truth

Believe the Truth

> *(know and memorize the truth)*

Live the Truth

> *(Love in Truth, Walk in Truth, Workers of Truth)*

Speak the Truth

  (To Others, In Confrontation, Against Strongholds)

Pray the Truth

Proclaim the Truth

Desire the Truth

Chapter 12: Absolute or Abstract Truth

It has been my experience that many involved in untruth (abstract truth) or even religions and cults, will avoid discussion or dialog of their views because of the insecurity of their beliefs. Seemingly, they believe what they believe, and they don't desire to find the truth. Synonyms for abstract are, non-concrete, irrelevant, inconsequential, and immaterial. One definition of abstract truth is "thought apart from concrete realities." I think any belief that can't stand up to debate or intellectual discussion is probably a flawed and weak belief at best. It is, however, their belief and they are entitled to it.

I have friends and family involved in differing religions than mine, and they never want to sit down and discuss what they actually believe. On occasion, I will have a knock on the door from one of the different religions, and if they don't know me, they will immediately begin presenting their beliefs to me. I will always be gracious and kind and listen to their presentation but, if I begin to challenge their teaching at all, it always seems that they, un-expectantly, need to leave. In fact, some beliefs demand that their "converts" not talk to anyone of a contrary belief. Truth should never be afraid to be tested; Truth will always stand the test!

Dr. Everett Piper, President of Oklahoma Wesleyan University said, "He who defines the terms, wins the debate." Dr. Piper is correct but to win a debate at the expense of truth can be fatal! It would be like debating the values of drinking, but not allowing a discussion on the lethal contents of arsenic when consumed. Truth matters!

To ensure a decent conversation, terms like respect for one another and control of one's anger are admirable ground rules but, to define the terms of truth is irresponsible and impossible! One can say there is no absolute truth, but they are deceiving themselves.

Baby boomers, probably the first demographic group to consider that truth might be debatable, are now watching the millennials completely embrace the lie!

In 2012, on one of my many trips to China, I met a French college student named David. He was volunteering as a summer help at an orphanage that my group had been involved with for fourteen years. One evening, we had an interesting discussion about absolute truth. David was reluctant at first but indulged me further as he learned of my connection with the orphanage. The discussion began in the early evening, and the midnight hour delayed further debate until the following afternoon when we inevitably met once again.

The conversation started over the "fate" of the children being orphaned, and his opinion that it was just that, fate! I, of course, felt that God knew everything about them, and had "a future and a hope" for them.

"for I know the plans that I have for you,' declares the Lord, 'plans for welfare and not for calamity to give you a future and a hope." (Jeremiah 29:11)

David immediately moved into a mild defense mode saying, "So, you're blaming God for the children's situation?" I contended that their situation was probably better than it would be in their own homes, considering many came from an abusive or alcoholic condition. I knew many of the children's backgrounds, David didn't. They had warm beds and three healthy meals a day in the orphanage. The children also had loving and compassionate care from the main orphanage staff, whom I knew well. Unlike most orphanages in China, this one was privately run. I had the opportunity several years before, to lead the lady owner to the Lord.

The conversation, with David, somehow evolved into "absolutes" with him saying, "I don't believe in absolutes at all! The statement itself was an absolute, so I humbly reminded him that according to his distinct standards, he didn't believe his own statement. He sheepishly agreed. Our debate was, in fact, constructive and friendly.

I welcomed the challenge, as did he, knowing that it could eventually strengthen or refine our convictions in the end.

Since David didn't believe in absolutes, we moved into the discussion of right or wrong. Not surprisingly, he didn't believe in right or wrong either. I was amazed when he mentioned that the children were not necessarily "better off" in the orphanage because "Who's to say what is right or wrong?" His statement stirred my demonstrative side! I immediately suggested an extreme, but fitting analogy; "What if your parents, heaven forbid, were murdered by an intruder into their home, it would be wrong would it not?" David's answer shocked me, "That is the intruder's choice, why should I question if it is right or wrong?"

I was beginning to see a pattern. I thought, "David's position on moral absolutes was not likely to alter, but what if I challenged him on physical absolutes instead?"

We were sitting on some steps on a narrow cobblestone street in the "old town" area of Lijiang, China. Surrounding us were two and three-story buildings with shops on the bottom floors, and residents' quarters on the upper floors. I asked David if he would go to the top of one of the buildings and jump off, to which he responded, "Of course not!" I asked him, "Why not?" He affirmed, "Because I would fall to the ground and be seriously injured or killed!" My reply was, "No, you would be ok because there are NO absolutes." David chuckled and said, "I do believe in gravity!" "So, you are acknowledging there are absolutes?" I asked. He agreed, "Yes, I believe there are some physical absolutes that have been proven scientifically." I questioned how science can "prove" anything if there are "no absolutes," but I didn't argue that point with him. I was just pleased that David acknowledged any absolutes at all!

David's story can be repeated over and over. Many intellectuals will not accept absolutes unless first proven (an absolute) with scientific evidence. Mental and spiritual absolutes may never have the scientific evidence which intellectuals demand but, that lack of evidence doesn't make mental and spiritual truth any less factual than physical absolutes like gravity! No one has ever seen air, for instance, but because we experience breathing it, we don't doubt its existence. Many people thought the Wright brothers were crazy when they envisioned large objects flying in the "invisible" air. Even though objects could fly, and aerodynamics was an absolute truth, the doubters and intellectuals of that day would not believe without the eventual proof.

The mathematical probability of Jesus fulfilling even eight of the Messianic prophecies is 1 in several trillion or 1 in 10^{17} power. Many studies have been done with these astronomical odds, but the fact is that Jesus fulfilled them all! Aside from the archaeological and written proof which is abundant, ample historical and political evidence is available as well. Just the fact that Jesus died and rose again, and His body has never been found in over two thousand years should be proof enough.

I'm convinced that the "right or wrong" and "abstracter's" motivation and doubt is much deeper than simply proving a truth scientifically or producing the evidence. The real disagreement comes when one is challenged in the area of spiritual truth!

I believe that no amount of "proof" will ever convince the intellectual of spiritual truth unless they are willing to admit that there is a God and that each of us is separated from God because of our sin. I believe that "Right or wrong" and "spiritual absolutes" are code for sin in the intellectual world. Man has a difficult time admitting sin because in doing so, it brings guilt, and therefore requires a response. However, if a man denies sin, and the existence of God, he will presumably escape the guilt. Many will conclude that there is no God simply because they cannot see Him. I still contend that the true reason for their motivation and belief is their excuse for doing what they really want to do, without the inconveniences of the guilt. Many want to live as they choose without guilt, subsequently, they need an excuse such as no "right or wrong." On the Mark Levin Show, Life, Liberty & Levin, Secularist David Berlinski, editor of International Review of Science humbly admitted that he, as a Secularist wanted to "Have a good time all the time." His observation was that secularists tend to "marginalize into smaller groups and are happy as long as their personal needs are met."

A Secular Humanist's foundation of belief is that; man is god and therefore man will eventually discover, through human effort and intellect, the answers to every question and dilemma that humans face. I would argue that those who advocate that there is no right or wrong, or that there are no absolutes, are secular humanists, if not in conviction, at least in philosophy!

Traveling on a flight from Chicago to Pittsburg, (as I referenced in chapter seven concerning divine appointments) and on my way to speak at a youth conference, my favorite seats on the plane (aisle seats near the front of the cabin) had all been taken. I am one that needs an occasional stroll, and I don't want to disturb passengers by crawling over them during a flight.

On this flight, I boarded a plane that was connecting with another incoming flight and the only seat available was a window seat just three rows back of the bulkhead. I thought, "The window is better than the middle seat, at least I can see out."

Seated just to my left, in the center, was a flight attendant, dressed in her uniform, and on the aisle seat to her left, a gentleman in a business suit. Typically, on full flights, most people are already talking and making conversation rather easily related to the full flights or the temperature of the plane, etc. On this particular flight, the conservation on my row was directed at the flight attendant as she explained that she was dead-heading to Pittsburg, to pick up another flight into New York City.

After the traditional flight instructions and take-off, the lady asked me where I was from and what I did as a profession. I told her that I was from Texas and was a student pastor on my way to speak at a conference in Pittsburg. Her reply was, "I'm a youth worker too!" She began to explain that she volunteered with the youth in her local Unitarian church. I thought, "This should be an interesting conversation." Then she asked, "What religion do you work with?" I answered, "The Christian religion." She then said, "What denomination?" I said, "Southern Baptist." She replied rather cynically, "Oh!" I asked her if she was disappointed. She said, "No, it's just that we probably don't believe the same." I agreed to say, "You are right, we probably don't, but that is one's privilege."

We discussed that Unitarian's believe man is essentially god and that eventually, through man, and the ingenuity of man, answers would be discovered to all difficult questions in life. My response, of course, was that all things were created by God and the existence of everything was from God. I didn't challenge her about the very science in which she put her trust, and that it had failed at so many points to prove many of its theories i.e., Evolution and the never found "missing link," and Carbon Dating based on unknown and unproven sources. In my opinion, establishing carbon dating techniques on a million-year-old tree, which no one ever witnessed, is hardly proof of that technique and its authenticity. Both theories have since been refined and they are just that, "theories," not facts!

Then she asked, "So if there is a God, how can He allow evil in the world?" I guess I could have said, "If man is god, then how can man allow evil in the world?" But I didn't. Instead, I asked if she was a parent. She began to light up as she described her delightful little three-year-old son, and how cute and wonderful he was. Then I told her that I had three sons and a daughter, and we were then able to enjoy together, the "wonderfulness" of our children for a few short minutes.

"To answer your question; 'If there is a God, how can He allow evil in the world?'" I explained if her son was anything like my sons they were cute, but like typical little boys, they were sometimes hard to corral for even a short disingenuous hug. She laughed and agreed with me. I told her that little boys would much rather be finding rocks and killing frogs than giving hugs to their parents. Then I explained that there were times (very seldom) that my son might take time out of his "frog killing" to voluntarily crawl up in my lap, give me a hug, and say, "I love you, Daddy!" Those were very special times. "He might even hang around on my lap and give me kisses for a few extra minutes if I was lucky!" I said.

Then I asked her, "What would you prefer; a forced hug when you snatch your son as he's running by on his way to a "frog killing" and pushing himself out of your arms, or a long, voluntary, sincere hug just because he chose to hug, out of his genuine love for you?" She said, "I would take either, but I prefer the voluntary hugs." I explained, "Me too, and that's why there is evil in the world. God wanted to give us a choice to love Him, and not force us to love Him! With choice, sin entered the world because man chose to go their own way."

The lady told me that, "God must not be very loving to allow sin to ruin people's lives." I said, "You would be correct had God not sent His Own Son, Jesus, to redeem us from that sin!" Later, I began to go through the Four Spiritual Laws, my favorite gospel tract, as she listened rather indifferently, but politely.

At the end of the presentation, there is always a prayer that one can pray to receive Christ as their personal Lord and Savior. I asked the lady if she would like to pray that prayer to receive Christ as her own personal Savior and Lord. She cynically replied, "No, I don't." During the presentation, I was so focused on the lady and her desire to know Christ, that I never even considered anyone else might be listening and that God might have a better plan.

The gentleman on the aisle then leaned forward and said, "Sir, I'll pray that prayer!" I looked at the flight attendant and asked, "Do you mind trading seats with this gentleman?" She reluctantly got up and slid to the aisle seat as the man took her place. I explained to the man that it isn't the prayer you pray, but the attitude of your heart that saves you. He understood. The entire time of talking with both the lady and the gentleman, I tried to keep it private and personal. I was trying to be sensitive to their privacy by not being loud and lurid.

We were at the point in the flight where the pilot pulls back the throttles, and as we approach the landing, all becomes quiet and subdued. I whispered quietly, "Ok sir, I will pray, and if you will pray the prayer after me." He said, "Ok." Quietly I said, "Lord Jesus, I need you." Then loudly and without shame, the man shouted, "LORD JESUS I NEED YOU!" He continued the prayer just that way and when he concluded he clapped his hands and said, "So I'm saved now?" I said, "Yes, sir you are!" Then I explained to him that I was sorry that I didn't have anything to give him to help him grow in his faith, and I wished I did. From over my left shoulder came the booklet, The Survival Kit by Ralph Neighbor. It is, in my opinion, one of the best follow-up tools to use for new Christians. It just so happened that the man behind me on the plane had one with him to give away. Nothing ever takes God by surprise (Divine appointments!)

I asked the lady if she wanted to reconsider but she said, "No!" I said, "I want you to keep this tract, and when you get to the point in your life that you realize that man is not the answer (and you will) I want you to reconsider receiving Christ." She put the tract in her purse and smiled. I still pray for the lady flight attendant to this day, and that she eventually received the Lord.

God pursues us! He doesn't hide from us or make us chase Him. He is like the loving Mommy or Daddy who desires to hold and love us even though we are solely intent on "frog killing!"

When we admit our sin and confess that Jesus Christ died for us, and rose again from the dead to intercede for us, that experience will initiate and carry on a relationship with the Creator of the universe! It will begin a life-changing process of truth and Divine appointments that can only be explained by God! And that is a fact!

The philosophy of both David, and the flight attendant, was that of Secular Humanism whether that was their intended philosophy or not. I am sure their beliefs were learned directly or indirectly from the culture they were exposed to which, obviously, had little ambition for truth.

TRUTH

Chapter 13: Deception of Truth in Our World

Comments I hear almost every day:

"I don't know who to believe anymore!"

"Our World is falling apart!"

"The families in America are being destroyed!"

"I can't go on anymore!"

"I don't know how much more of this I can take!"

"The sky is falling; the sky is falling!"

The sky may not be falling yet, but are we at a point of no return unless someone intervenes?

Listed in the first paragraph of this chapter, are some of the questions many are asking, maybe not openly, but secretly inside their hearts as the events all around us seem to be out of control.

We see world events crashing in around us, and if that's not bad enough, our families and friends are facing astronomical challenges as well. We look at ourselves and we feel discouraged, or depressed, or angry, or confused or any number of other emotions and feelings, and we ask, "When is this going to stop?"

Believe it or not, there are answers and solutions to all the questions everyone is asking. We may feel inadequate to resolve many of these questions, especially those on a grander scale that may involve legislation and political resolutions, but there are solutions to our personal struggles and battles of fear, or depression, and any "stronghold" that may have us stonewalled and defeated.

I remember hearing as a young man; my parents, my coaches, and teachers all saying, "You are only responsible for you! You can't worry about everyone else, but you can take care of you!" I have even explained to young people, who live in very difficult situations, that they can make good choices. I truly believe, even in the most difficult situations, that the personal choices we make determine our future regardless of our past or current circumstances.

Joseph is the perfect Biblical illustration of making good choices in difficult situations. Joseph dreamed that he would rule; yet he was sold into slavery by his brothers, wrongly accused of sexual misconduct, and erroneously imprisoned but, in all these circumstances, he did the right thing. What seemed to be a step down with each situation was in fact, a step up and an opportunity for God to move Joseph into power, just as he had dreamed. What a surprise to his brothers when they found themselves bowing to Joseph, their new leader. God was not surprised!

Many of our poor choices come from misinformed resources. We listen to, and believe, statements and philosophies which may, at their core, have a false or untrue premise. This is sometimes why we fall into depression or become fearful, and we allow our feelings to begin deceiving us, rather than seeking the truth.

These personal emotions are only aggravated and intensified when we see all the other "soap operas" going on around us. There is always more than one way to see or do anything yet, we choose to remain trapped in the quagmire of lies.

Like Joseph, I believe when we examine, pursue, and follow truth, we will begin to see our personal, political, and spiritual lives return to the order in which they were meant to be. I am not saying that life will be perfect, of course, it won't be, but I am saying we will begin restoration and healing that is so desperately needed and will bring honor to God.

Truth, no matter where it is bent or twisted, needs to be exposed and restored. We need to know world and domestic "lies" that really, to a large extent, add to many of our family and personal dilemmas.

Maybe if we learn to take care of our personal needs, and begin the truth process at home, then it will affect the world around us.

I'm sure many are thinking, "what about end-time predictions and the eventual demise of our world?" I know that we will see "nation against nation, brother against brother, disobedience to parents" etc. but the Church, and more specifically, the Christian has been given the mandate to be salt and light to the world. In those difficult situations, it is not the time for the Church to retreat, but rather, is time for the Church to be the salt and light that is so desperately needed.

Our world is, and has been changing morally, politically, and spiritually for several years. It is the responsibility of the Church to change, not doctrinally, but to change its methods in reaching our world. So far, that task has been like pushing a sitting elephant down the road. Fortunately, the Church is beginning to wake up and see the need, it is slow and painful in some respects, but it is beginning to happen. The church's deficiency of influence over the past generation is becoming much more obvious as we see the decline in morals and values in our world.

We need to take each situation and know that the choices we make, no matter our circumstances, are very important as I mentioned. Our personal choices can make a big difference in our lives.

Aside from our personal choices, it important for each of us to call for change in our society as well. The Parkland Florida school shootings have empowered many, including children, to call for gun law changes, and even for the removal of the second amendment! "If you see something, say something," has been touted by others as an important tool, and even mental health issues have been debated. In respect to "see something, say something," the "Starbucks" incident where two Black men sat, for a long time, in the establishment without ordering anything stirred suspicion. The young worker felt the need to "say something" but paid dearly for doing so. Our politically correct world begs for consistency!

When our politicians begin to defend MS-13 gangs who rape, murder, behead, and dis-member young innocent girls, then we know that truth has lost its way!

Some of the discussion, as mentioned above, is no doubt helpful, but none of the suggestions that I've listed are the solution to eliminating the violence. Again, we see the left *using* students to further their agenda to disarm America. The left is very good at finding ways to involve the students, even on school time! I wonder if a pro-life demonstration were planned during school hours if the media would praise the students involved just as they have the gun demonstrators? "Whoever wants this generation the most will get them!" –Unknown.

Let's be honest, shootings, rape, domestic violence, bombings, bullying, divorce, physical abuse, alcoholism, and drug abuse to name a few of this nation's problems, are still with us!

America has made stronger laws, it's invested millions of dollars, offered more and more institutions to help allevi- ate these ills, and yet they remain!

America seems afraid of the obvious answer, but we will continue to politicize these issues for the sake of political brownie points, and at the expense of fallen students and a destroyed nation!

In all the debates of the past several years, I have only heard one or two voices of TRUTH! The latest voice was Baltimore Raven player Benjamin Watson when he told Fox News' anchor, Martha MacCallum "The answer is God!" Watson went on to explain the influence of God in his life and home growing up. He cited it as the main reason his life is where it is today.

Yes, the problems need multiple solutions, and we need to look reasonably at any, and all possible effective answers but, gun laws, education, and even armed guards will never mend the moral and ethical source of a sinful heart. All so- lutions begin with God!

We have allowed any influence of God to be removed from our public schools and have gone to the extreme of even forcing coaches to refrain from prayer on the field of play. Our schoolbooks no longer contain any religious reference to our Christian founding as a nation nor religious statements by our brave founding forefathers.

Public display of manger scenes or any form of religious activity is more and more detached from our society, and we wonder why these tragic events happen.

I will expound more on the deliberate dismantling of America in chapter 15, but until we return to the TRUTH behind our moral demise as a country, we will continue to see our society decline. The Bible gives us clear instruction on a way forward, and it's addressed to Christians!

(If) My people who are called by My name humble themselves and pray and seek My face and turn from their wicked ways, then I will hear from heaven, will forgive their sin, and will heal their land. (2 Chronicles 7:14)

God is not expecting non-believers to do the right thing, He is pleading for Christians, those who know Christ as their Savior and Lord, those who know the TRUTH, to humble themselves and PRAY, and turn from their wicked ways.

"THEN," our land will be healed! It's not guns or gun laws. It's not protests or legislation, or political debate, It's Christians! When Christians stop complaining about the music, or the color of their carpet, or the length of the sermon and start sincerely seeking God in prayer, things will change!

When it's your son or daughter that is tragically killed or your church that's terrorized, then maybe true prayer and soul searching will begin. What will it take Church, for us to humble ourselves and PRAY, instead of pointing fingers, and alleging blame?

Truth in our World begins with Christians!

Chapter 14: The Decline of Truth Politically

Our nation was known for bravery, honesty, ingenuity, morality, and generosity; just a few of the adjectives which described the character of a country built from a passionate desire for freedom! Although history records many brave acts on the part of our founding fathers, in fighting for that freedom, few of them would expound on their own bravery.

"We hold these truths to be self-evident, that all men are created equal, that they are endowed by their Creator with certain unalienable Rights, that among these are Life, Liberty and the pursuit of Happiness." –The Declaration of Independence

I'm concerned that if our present course doesn't change quickly, America will descend into obscurity much like the Roman Empire. Many will laugh at the suggestion that America, "the greatest country in the world," will have a similar demise as did the Roman Empire, but I argue that we've already begun to descend.

Not only do I believe that America is descending, but I believe an organized and intentional movement is under way to minimize the power and success of this country.

Globalization is the goal of many progressives which is designed to bring America into universal thinking. As much as I enjoy the Olympics, it too is being used as a political tool to influence a one-world rationale. Yes, we need to love one another as the Olympics suggest, but a deeper purpose is no doubt intended. What used to be a not so obvious plan of our demise has, in recent years, become more apparent. Even the obvious has still deceived many because of their apathy and naivety to the truth.

Our strengths, in many ways, have become our weaknesses. The enemy knows the tendencies of the American people to trust its leaders, even when that trust is sometimes challenged. Our trust was obvious in the FBI, but the need for accountability has become much more apparent in recent months. Our legacy of honesty and integrity has always given people the benefit of the doubt, a second chance, and a willingness to forgive. Because of our forgiving spirit as a nation, it is sometimes easy for the enemy to slowly "slither" in with change, frequently exploiting children, and their perils as a disguise for their true motives.

For example, The Left was trying to persuade Americans, during the Obama presidency to allow the arguably, Illegal enactment of a Presidential Edict (Executive Orders) on Immigration; citing all the heartache it would cause the "children" of illegal Immigrants, who might be separated from their families, if not enacted.

Who wouldn't want to help children, after all this is America! Everyone has a heart for children and hates to see them exploited. The fact is; two constitutional laws would've been broken or at least stretched to allow one unconstitutional Presidential Edict! The truth, in this situation, would be to follow the law and require the families to go back home together and enter the country legally concerning the current immigration laws. Some concessions would need to be ironed out by congress concerning more technical cases like "birthers," but the law needs to be followed. Holding employers accountable for hiring illegals would start a natural and voluntary process of return for many who don't have U.S. Visas or Green Cards. I am for mercy in many cases, but the rule of law cannot be ignored! The neglect, and lack of enforcement of existing law, has exacerbated the current situation, and has fashioned congress into cowardly politicians!

In my opinion, the true motivation for the illegal Edict was not to help the children as much, as to ultimately shift the leftist voting bloc in its favor. Many are saying the illegals couldn't vote anyway, but I am convinced, we would soon hear the cry for their right to vote not long afterward. Illinois is in the process of issuing I. D's to illegals which would allow them the authorization to vote in that state!

Federal voting laws and especially consistent identification guidelines need critical changes. Only legitimate and verifiable citizens should be voting in American elections! The argument, for too long, has been that voter identification alienates and inconveniences minorities and the poor when in fact, everyone needs identification to drive, travel or own a house. The protests come only on voting rights, and purely for political reasons.

It's hard to understand the left's outcry over Russia's interference with elections when at the same time, they are advocating the right for illegals to vote! How much more two-faced can one get?

However, the shift of the voting bloc doesn't require the illegals to vote or even be citizens, but rather, uses the population increase in strong democratic districts to insure a larger electoral number and more democratic electoral votes. Presidential elections are won by electoral votes, not the popular vote. The population of states is based on headcount regardless of legal or illegal status. Proposed changes to the new census form are proof of the Left's need to keep illegal's identity secret.

Irrespective of the political ramifications, the flood of illegal immigrants and especially the Syrian refugees are, in my opinion, a Trojan horse for America. If this action continues and the refugees are freely allowed to enter our nation, this is a tragedy waiting to happen in this country! The core values of America will be changed, almost overnight much like that of Sweden. I truly hope with all my heart that I am mistaken. The core values on which this country was founded, cannot be allowed to be changed by overnight mass immigration and illegal refugees. Immigration laws were enacted for this very reason.

On a similar issue related to increasing the voting bloc, President Obama's administration floated the idea of passing legislation; forcing citizens to vote or be fined! I certainly don't want the "uninformed" voter to be FORCED to vote! Why don't we just go ahead and allow children to vote too? Because they are UNINFORMED! Some voters know less than children about the issues, yet it's been alleged that many "uninformed" voters have been bussed in, and some of them were even PAID to vote! No one would want an untrained or unskilled worker building their new home, yet we allow, and even bribe, in some cases, uninformed voters to "re-build" America.

Liberals are encouraging "rights" for those who illegally entered our country, but illegals should have to earn those "rights," as did those who demonstrated the integrity and respect for American values, to enter the country through proper immigration! Sadly, I am almost certain that a large percentage of "legal" Americans, if asked to pass the immigration test, would fail miserably! I'm not suggesting that we test the voter before elections, which would be absurd, but I am saying that we need to strongly encourage the voter to inform themselves on the issues and candidates before voting…a principle which the left doesn't embrace.

Something else to consider is the change that illegal immigration will bring to the face of America, including the H-1B Visa that President Obama introduced during his last term, and our new "conservative" congress seemed to be allowing! The H-1B Visa, as I understand it, is a work visa that allows one hundred thousand Middle Eastern tech workers, as well as thousands of other foreign workers that don't share the same traditions and values as most Americans, to enter the country and take away, what should be American citizen's jobs! What Illegal immigration has done to eliminate lower-paying unskilled jobs for Americans, the H-1B visa does to destroy thousands of higher-paying jobs for skilled and trained workers. The rationale given; companies can pay foreign workers lower salaries, with little or no benefits (benefits that the government requires for American workers). I think this endeavor was another deliberate attempt to "fundamentally change America."

If government regulations were removed, then companies wouldn't need foreign labor. I believe that liberal government uses the "regulations" as political talking points;

"look what I've done for you," and then, points to the high cost of labor to allow for more foreign workers, which again, bolsters the electoral numbers.

The TPP (Trans-Pacific Partnership) Agreement, which Congress and President Obama seemed to be aligning on, had hidden immigration regulations in Chapter 10 that would exempt most current and future regulations to allow for foreign workers, and their *families*, to enter the country on a fast-track plan bypassing normal immigration laws. This is unconscionable! This agreement alone could "fundamentally change the United States of America!" Fortunately, the Trump administration has sidelined this issue for now, but its future is still being considered.

More government always leads to more dependency, which leads to what I like to refer to as, the "Mugabe factor," and the people are, therefore, at the mercy of the government. Many view government programs as free, but seem to forget that they are actually paying for them with increased tax revenue!

The movement to change America is no longer slowly "slithering," but has gained legs, and has a prominent voice of which to promote a "fundamental change of the United States of America!" No longer is it a slow and unassuming movement, but it has become loud, forceful, and powerful, and if we the people don't wake up, it will be too late to reverse!

One needs only to study the fall of Zimbabwe, Africa, as orchestrated by President Robert Mugabe, whom I mentioned previously, to see the almost carbon copy deceit confronting America. It was cunningly designed for the eventual dictatorship of a once democratic, and wealthy, diamond-rich African nation.

Some will argue that Zimbabwe is still democratic and still holds free elections. What most of the world doesn't see are the Mugabe thugs (the militarized police forces) raiding villages before the June elections, and cutting off the hand of the youngest child in the village, as an example of what will happen if Mugabe is not reelected! The demise of Zimbabwe, as argued by many Americans living there at the time, was begun with the promise of free government programs and welfare, and then climaxed with the overhaul and assurance of healthcare for all. Government control!

After the free or nearly free programs instituted by Mugabe's administration were established, which caused a dependency on the government, it was then, that the corrupt but seemingly compassionate government slowly removed guns from the people and hindered their ability to defend themselves. All this came, of course, as the army and local police departments were federally regulated to benefit the government of Zimbabwe's purposes and eventual takeover of the country. The news media was ultimately government-controlled as well, which allowed only the propaganda of the corrupt administration.

As recently as the South Texas church shooting, and the Los Vegas rampage; liberals have been calling, once again, for guns to be severely limited because of their "cause" for violence and death. The responsibility for the shootings lies solely on the person, not the gun, but it doesn't fit the liberal narrative or eventual objective of the liberal government to ultimately control American citizens.

We don't see the outcry for the removal of alcohol which causes, on average, 88,000 deaths a year as opposed to almost 32,000-gun deaths a year, of which, 20,000 were suicides or accidents (Simple Facts and Plane Arguments 1/16/2013). As recently as Christmas Eve 2015, President Obama vowed executive action in early 2016 saying, "That's especially true for one piece of unfinished business, that's our epidemic of gun violence." He later said in that weekly press conference that the action would be taken to "protect our kids from gun violence." Almost 33,000 children (20 years and younger) die each year because of alcohol-related causes, but no outcry to remove alcohol at all is ever heard from our liberal legislators.

Children are frequently the object of any legislation or liberal agenda, as a tool to pull the heartstrings of the American public. Yet, when alcohol kills more children than guns, it's always the individual's fault and the abuse of the alcohol, rather than the alcohol itself. Alcohol serves no political agenda for the left, so there is little attention given to it. Guns, on the other hand, serve as a protection against a renegade regimen, and the last stronghold leading to a socialist or tyrant government. The second amendment gives U.S. citizens the right to "keep and bear arms" but this amendment is being challenged every day with little regard to the responsibility of the offender, but rather with the emphasis on the gun as though it shoots itself.

When guns are taken from the people; and this was part of the "fundamental change of America," which Mr. Obama advocated, then the people will have little or no recourse against a renegade government! WE would be relegated to sticks and rocks in any attempt to take our government back just as we have seen in Iran and Iraq in the past.

None of the proposed liberal gun law changes would have prevented most of the recent incidents, when in fact; Chicago, for instance, boasts one of the strongest gun laws in the nation, yet records the highest gun violence. The only suggested solution, of course, is to eliminate guns, altogether, which is not a legitimate solution but is the ultimate goal of the liberal left.

It could be reasonably argued that much of the crime is carried out because tips are being withheld from people who are afraid to report suspicious activity, simply because of being labeled as "Racists." That was the case, at least, with the neighbor in the San Bernardino, California shooting, and could explain many other cases because of our "politically correct" climate.

With the death of Justice Antonin Scalia and the suspicious lack of forensics surrounding it, doubts were raised as to the truth of his demise.

Considering the teetering condition of the Supreme Court, and the pending cases that were waiting in the wings such as; voting districts in Texas which could tilt the decision toward the Democrats, religious liberty which requires employers, under the Affordable Care Act (Obama Care) to provide birth control, and abortion restrictions, proposed by Texas on women's healthcare clinics, a huge threat to Roe v. Wade, the suspicions of Justice Scalia were reasonably justified.

Replacing a strict constitutionalist with a liberal or even moderate Justice would radically change the make-up of the court and eventually the face of America as we know it. The Supreme Court is just one more target for the liberal left to conquer in their "fundamental change." President Trump's appointment of Justice Neil Gorsuch has slightly balanced the court, but further retirements are looming with uncertainty ahead. Judges are needed who will properly interpret the law and not make law, which is the function of Congress, not judges!

Because of the trust of the American people, since our founding and beyond, we have allowed the truth to be defined differently, in recent years, by a liberal agenda. We have seen the "standard" change and adjust to the point of which there is no standard at all! If there is no standard or absolute, then we have diminished truth! Truth has been obstructed for the sake of personal gain politically, globally, scholastically, ethically, and even spiritually.

It was because of standards of trust, integrity, fairness, loyalty, patriotism, sacrifice, honesty, and devotion that our nation became and remained strong. We have allowed laziness instead of hard work, selfishness instead of sacrifice, and deception instead of transparency and honesty to permeate our lives. Truth has become blurred, at best, and we have raised entire generations who have learned compromise, dishonesty, selfishness, and government handouts as the pathway to success.

We need to return to the standard which made this nation great and begin to seek and know the truth, as passionately as did our forefathers before us. The intentional destruction of truth permeates business, government, media, education, entertainment, religion, family, and every other aspect of our lives. This begs for those who know the truth, to be as passionate and deliberate to proclaim it, as are those who are determined to destroy it!

The church, for too long, has ignored these seven cultural areas of influence; business, government, media, education, entertainment, religion, and family, and we are now paying the price as our culture becomes more secular and immoral every day.

Many refuse to know the truth or even practice what truth they do know. I hope you will have an openness to inspect the possibility that truth and absolutes do exist, and they can change your life! Others of you may feel that you have always believed in truth but might admit that you have become lax and uninformed, and maybe your tendency to trust has allowed undesired change to creep in.

The *principle of truth,* which was so vividly revealed to my wife and me several years ago, has changed our lives!

I will expound more on the social and political consequences, but the personal struggles of truth, are those with which all of us battle, and is what I have focused on in this book. All the aspects of truth are important which is why I write about them. However, it is with the personal struggles that we all contend and they most concern me and give reason to address them as the emphasis of the book. All areas of truth, social, political, and spiritual, affect one another, they are building blocks, and they are why each area has been addressed to some degree.

I know I cannot convince everyone of the truth which I write, but I ask only that you consider the possibility that maybe you too have not seen clearly, a principle that does exist, and that could revolutionize your life as it did mine!

The decline of truth politically is only one area where the enemy has attacked. With political influence, the enemy gains legal permission to thrive. The enemy, however, has gained, as I mentioned earlier, influence not only politically, but educationally as a base to teach, and form their ideals, by alleging "intolerance" to immoral lifestyles, and socially by enlisting media and entertainment to put a pleasant face on it. The family, and increasingly the Church, is becoming more open to the demise by simply doing nothing. Because the Church is becoming ignorant to the truth, they too have been deceived by the lie. In many cases, it's because the Church doesn't want to be labeled as "intolerant," so they mistakenly ignore the truth.

The Church is labeled "intolerant" when we don't accept values that directly contradict our beliefs, but the world is "progressive" and loving when they try to force their beliefs and practices on the Church. This is a result of the world, rather than the Church, gaining influence in the media, political, and other key areas of our society.

Many denominations of the Christian faith have, in fact, compromised and diluted their beliefs, and Biblical truths under the pressure of "intolerance." For these denominations, the appeal of tolerance has trumped truth and made them nothing more than a religious country club. They have waved the "white flag" in surrender to Satan's cunning plan.

Politics has found another victim in churches too weak to stand for the truth of God's word. Compromise is good when done out of a need to better a cause, but NEVER at the cost of truth!

TRUTH

Chapter 15: The Truth about Secular Humanism

It has become clear, in recent years; that is, *The Truth About Secular Humanism.*

"For they exchanged the truth of God for a lie and worshiped and served the creature rather than the Creator, who is blessed forever. Amen." (Romans 1:25)

Maybe you know little or nothing about Secular Humanism, but I want to expose a movement that is intent on changing America, and not for the better! America, what used to be a culture of faith with a basic Christian background or at least a respect for religion, has slowly been manipulated into more of a humanistic philosophy?

John J. Dunphy, Humanist magazine 1983: "Humanism is a religion with mankind as its god." He said, "Which will replace the rotting corpse of Christianity."

I first became aware of this movement in 1984 but after some investigation, I discovered that Secular Humanism (the philosophy that life's tough questions are found and resolved through human intellect) actually began as early as the 1930s. It theoretically began, of course, at the Tower of Babel.

A goal was set to reach zero population growth by the year 2000 which would enable the secular humanists to have fewer people on earth to influence with their message. Although the goal was missed, the pursuit continues. Zero population basically meant that the birth rate needed to decline, and the death rate needed to increase as they targeted seven essential areas.

The humanists not only targeted the population growth but also focused on, as I mentioned earlier, seven strategic areas of life, which they knew were essential to change, in order to fully "replace the rotting corpse of Christianity." Again, the essential areas included were **media**; who would become their voice, **education**; targeted to reach the youth, **entertainment**; designed to put an acceptable and legitimate "face" on their movement, **political**; for legislative and legal change, **financial**; to underwrite their movement, **family**; to transform moral and traditional values, **religion**; and more specifically, Christianity, their ultimate target, and purveyors of truth.

Interestingly, Christianity is the focus of Secular Humanism with little or no regard for other beliefs such as Islam, Buddhism, or Hinduism. I believe the reason is simple; Satan hates Jesus and the Christian religion that He represents! It makes sense then, that Satan's battle would be against his enemy. Satan doesn't need to battle that which isn't TRUTH! His battle is, and always has been, against God and His Son Jesus, the only *risen* Savior!

It should be evident, even in the recent world events, that most of the Middle Eastern countries are now aligning against Israel (the origin of Jesus and Christianity) and even Russia and China are preparing to strengthen themselves militarily in that respect. The books of Daniel and Revelation, in the Bible, thoroughly address this subject of world events.

A classroom situation would be the best way to illustrate the Humanist's Global 2000 goal of zero population growth. The idea was and remains, that if a teacher, for instance, had twenty students in a classroom and was teaching a principle or philosophy, it wouldn't be long before the teacher could possibly persuade the students of his or her beliefs. However, if that classroom added ten students to its number, at the six months period, the teacher would then need to back up and convince the newer students, of that which they had already taken six months to teach the original group.

Slowing the world population growth would result in fewer people to indoctrinate, and to do it in a shorter period of time. It is obvious to me that the Secular Humanists' plan has been enormously effective. Humanists; eliminating the population for sake of promoting their belief, is in direct contrast to the Christian philosophy of reaching every *living person* with the truth of Christ *before* they die!

Secular Humanists have as their primary target, the young and moldable mind; which demonstrates their patience and systematic plan to reach their goals. A famous man once declared, "Who controls the youth, controls the future." That man was Adolph Hitler, and he knew if he could control the youth of Germany, he would eventually control the future of Germany. We are now seeing students, used as pawns, to promote gun control and to indoctrinate them with a socialist view, wokeism, and gender discussions during school hours!

The shrinking population plan would be accomplished by secular Humanists in several ways.

To reduce the population, abortion was promoted along with birth control, family planning (two or fewer children), and an emphasis on environmental concerns. You may ask, "What do environmental concerns have to do with population control?" Global warming and the environmental emphasis has been used as a motivation; sighting "overcrowding" as the main contributor to the pollution and destruction of the planet! While I agree that we humans need to take care of our planet, we are not the primary contributor to its destruction. Natural occurrences such as one volcanic eruption, as argued by scientist Ian Plimer, could contribute more CO_2 "pollution" than would the total environmental conservation efforts of many years! Some argue that CO_2 is not a pollutant at all, but rather a necessary element for survival. "Over the past 250 years, humans have added just one part of CO_2 in 10,000 to the atmosphere. One volcanic "cough" can do this in a day." (Ian Plimer, The Drum TV, August 13, 2009)

Hardly a day passes that I don't see an ad targeting children with environmental messages. Watch some of the popular children's programs, just once, as I did with my grandsons recently, and you will see environmental advertisements and related program content throughout a significant portion of the shows.

The creature has become more important than the Creator! "for they exchanged the truth of God for a lie and worshiped and served the creature rather than the Creator, who is blessed forever." (Romans 1:25)

To further expand the Global 2000 agenda, The Pro-Choice and feminist movements have both contributed largely to the deaths of the unborn, and the birth control emphasis. The two movements have greatly reduced the population among Anglo Americans. Medicaid, to the chagrin of Humanists, has done the opposite among minority groups, and more recently Anglo girls, encouraging unwed mothers to have more children, a result of free Government welfare. These examples are again opposite to the truth of God's word!

"God blessed them; and God said to them, 'Be fruitful and multiply, and fill the earth, and subdue it; and rule over the fish of the sea and over the birds of the sky and over every living thing that moves on the earth.'" (Genesis 1:28)

An interesting side note: It is the Muslim religion that views a high birth rate as part of their means to accomplish world domination, while Christian birth rates are quickly decreasing in part, due to the "overcrowding" myth.

Another part of the Global 2000 plan was to embrace Homosexuality. The gay and lesbian agenda was cheered by humanists because children were not born to a homosexual union, and it also further deteriorated the idea of traditional family values as paramount. This particular strategy has affected me personally for numerous reasons; I have several friends and former students, whom I love dearly, that have chosen this lifestyle. I will continue to love them and involve myself in their lives as much as they will allow, but I cannot disregard God's word and His conclusions concerning the homosexual lifestyle.

While the homosexual's motives may be noble in their minds, the Secular Humanist's intentions of the movement were two-fold; One, to decrease population growth, and two, to change how society viewed traditional family values and morals. Both goals have been largely successful and accepted. While the gay and lesbian community championed equality, the Secular Humanists championed moral and numerical decline, and have used the LGBT community as a political and social pawn.

For Secular Humanists, when considering population reduction; every possibility, whether morally accepted or not, was examined as a viable option, including suicide. Remember, traditional morals and values were an enemy to population reduction. Suicide was argued by Secular Humanists as a personal right and choice of an individual, and society should adjust their view when judging this choice. "Medical Suicides" were encouraged as a means to relieve pain and suffering of both physical and psychological battles, and by reducing the senior adult population (euthanasia) who promoted traditional morals and values. By touting this philosophy, it has contributed to numerous deaths a year and further diminished the population, accomplishing the humanists' goal.

Using sensitivity training exercises in classrooms, humanists help to devalue moral choices with situational drills such as "Lifeboat." Lifeboat places eight kids in a circle and challenges them to eliminate three people because, only food enough for five people is available. Scenarios using an older man, a pregnant girl, and a famous scientist, for instance, ask the kids to choose one to eliminate. Most will choose the older man to be eliminated because he has lived a longer life. The pregnant girl was spared because she was representing two lives, and the scientist was needed because of his important research. The better choice, of course, would be to save everyone! Every life is valuable, but that choice is never an option; it doesn't fit the humanist philosophy or blueprint.

While Suicide contributed to the deaths of a mostly younger population, euthanasia was encouraged as a humane alternative to lying aimlessly in a nursing home or hospital bed and draining the Medicare system unnecessarily. A second reason for euthanasia was to eliminate those who held to traditional morals and values (senior adults) and lessen their influence on the next generation. This idea aligned with the second motivation given by Secular Humanists for the emphasis on the homosexual movement, and that was to change traditional morals and values.

Other efforts to promote the humanist philosophy were those of limiting competition (everyone is a winner) and to challenge patriotism in schools by imposing apathy and disinterest in traditional values. Recent American flag protests attest to this concern. The movement began to target education as the perfect place or platform to implement their teaching. Humanists' declared their first victory when primary school books were confirmed non-didactic (amoral) in 1984.

The 1983 'Humanist' magazine: "I am convinced that the battle for humankind's future must be waged and won in the public-school classroom by teachers that correctly perceive their rolls as proselytes of the new faith." —John J. Dunphy

Textbooks began, as early as the seventies, suggesting that old and outdated ideas about religion and moral values needed a new and more sensible point of view. Prentice-Hall's *Behind the Mask: Our Psychological World* (1972 p. 61) "It is thought-provoking to carry creativity training to its ultimate extreme, as at least one author has done. He suggests that if we truly want to induce completely creative thinking, we should teach children to question the Ten Commandments, patriotism, the two-party system, monogamy, and the laws against incest"

Humanists targeted and won seats on larger state school boards such as Texas and California, knowing the influence these states had on book publishers nationwide. Their goal was to change textbooks and school library books to a more Humanist and amoral philosophy. Judy Blume is a Humanist author, whom the movement touted and supported as a standard for school library books.

Award programs and promotions were encouraged, in school libraries, using suggested reading lists of humanist authors such as Blume. School libraries were encouraged to evaluate and purge books to reflect state requirements based on a non-didactic philosophy, or risk budget cuts to their program.

Secular Humanists were able to declare victory concerning library books as indicated by their claim in Humanist magazine.

Humanist magazine January 1984 "We have already won the battle for library books in secondary schools, none of the books are didactic (moral)."

As an indication of the success of apathy and American disloyalty, ask any students today who won the civil war and answers will vary from, "I don't know," to "Germany?" A systematic dismantling of American morals and values and loyalty to *anything* is slowly but surely taking place. Mr. Trump had it right, make America great again!

American students are being encouraged to think more globally, with a tolerance of different governments and traditions. They are challenged to have an open mind to world philosophies (world view) and values suggesting a movement toward a one-world government. Even efforts to establish a unified world monetary system are quickly advancing. Complications with the Euro slowed progress somewhat but has been a prolific experiment and pathway to the world currency.

According to USA Today's, Joe McDonald, AP Business Writer says, "China is calling for a global currency to replace the dominant dollar." In 2013, David Lee Miller reported for Fox News, about a plan by the United Nations for a world currency. How close we are to that world currency is not clear, but discussions in many circles continue toward that end.

Not only have primary and secondary schools been reasonably indoctrinated, but colleges and universities are now being marketed as glowing examples of the changing "tolerance" movement. It's no wonder that the political left is promoting free college education and loan forgiveness. The humanist movement is applauding this proposal, and why not! Just imagine, not only is the typical college or university espousing the humanist philosophy but now the left wants the government to finance it!

An astute perception of universities was made by Oklahoma Wesleyan University, President, Dr. Everett Piper; "**Uni**versity not **Di**versity!" His point, as I understood it, was that America should be focused on our common strengths rather than our differences. Hasn't that been the cry of our African American community for years?

Dr. Martin Luther King Jr. cited the "American creed" in his famous "I have a dream" speech. He said, "We hold these truths to be self-evident, that all men are created equal." He continued that his children should, "not be judged by the color of their skin but by the content of their character." Yet in recent years the opposite cry of diversity has been championed and what seemed to be the realization of Dr. King's "dream" coming true, has begun a quick descent in the opposite direction. Those who once promoted humanity, and unity, are now radically advocating diversity and tolerance. Ethnicity, skin color, and gender have alienated America back into groups rather than "one nation."

Balkanization is the fragmentation of hostile regions in the world, The Balkans, and many African regions. These regions of disintegration were continuously in "tribal wars" with no resolution in sight. America and the rhetoric of diversity over unity will eventually fracture our country if we don't soon rediscover our strength; "one nation under God." Because of our unity, even though we are diverse, America has flourished! I believe the "diversity" movement is politically encouraged and motivated. The truth be known, the "descent" is being funded by liberal hate groups and rich entrepreneurs who want to stir up the controversy for political gain. College campuses have become the breeding ground for this hate; hence the reason liberals wanted the government to fund universities.

The federal government was established to defend and protect its people, not to totally finance our lives! Of course, the more that government is involved in our lives, the more we surrender to its control.

The movement has succeeded in changing the morals of our society and has promoted the idea of no absolutes. It's not my intention to prove the success of the secular humanist movement but to show, however, that there is a battle between truth and evil. Plenty of data is available to prove my point including the Humanist Manifesto I and II, but proof of evil is not the purpose of this book.

It is important to see how truth has been attacked and that Satan is in full battle mode against the truth. Our children no longer have the positive influences that were once in our homes, schools, and even churches. My attempt in this book has been to show the importance of truth, and that truth is also the most important thing to God.

Our battle is not with liberals, conservatives, ethnic groups, or genders, but with Satan, who "comes to steal, kill, and destroy!"

"And you will know the truth, and the truth will make you free." (John 8:32)

Truth is the answer to conflict, addictions, freedom, and the struggles that both the churched and unchurched are experiencing. I am writing with the assumption that you, the reader, already believe that there is truth. The important thing; how do we apply truth in our lives, and what does truth have to do with our happiness and joy?

I cannot convince anyone about the *truth* of God and the relationship which he desires to have with us. It is the power of the Holy Spirit that draws one to God, and convicts of sin and rebellion to Him.

"No one can come to Me unless the Father who sent Me draws him; and I will raise him up on the last day." (John 6:44)

The truths shared here, are mostly spiritual and not likely proven by scientific means, but rather experienced by those responsive to the teaching and ministry of the Holy Spirit.

The "Truth Principle," is that which is born out of searching, seeking, and listening to God. The principle was always available in God's word, but I believe He revealed it to my wife and me at the time we needed it most.

"For the word of God is living and active and sharper than any two-edged sword, and piercing as far as the division of soul and spirit, of both joints and marrow, and able to judge the thoughts and intentions of the heart." (Hebrews 4:12)

The Bible is God's *living* word! It is always speaking to us, convicting us, and teaching us. It is *active*! The Holy Spirit brings the Word alive to those of us who know Christ as Savior and Lord. To those who've not received Christ as Savior, reading the Word may be equivalent to that of one reading someone else's love letter. While reading another's love letter might be interesting, the content will probably not evoke the same emotion as it would to the proper recipient to whom it is written. In the same way, "God's word will not return void," but unbeliever's reading the Word, apart from the Holy Spirit, will not experience the intended result. That's not to say that the Word of God will not convict a non-believer and bring him to the saving knowledge of Jesus Christ…It can and has done so.

"...and you will know the truth, and the truth will make you free." (John 8:32)

Again, I cannot convince anyone of the truth, but when one *knows* the truth, the truth will set you free!

We are living in a time where truth is distorted and even those who lead us can hardly be trusted to speak the truth. We are told one thing and later find out something else to be true. Our ambassador in Benghazi was murdered and dragged through the streets yet, the facts were being hidden from the American people. Bowe Bergdahl, supposedly captured by ISIS and traded for five *known* terrorist detainees in GITMO, was full of cover-up! According to Lt. Col. Michael Waltz, in charge of the Bergdahl search, where six American soldiers lost their lives, Bergdahl, was being sought as a "deserter!" The five GITMO terrorists, chosen by ISIS, were *all* Generals, overseeing important areas including intelligence, training, and strategy as noted by Brigadier General Tony Tata on *Fox News' Hannity*.

I believe that leadership, no matter the political party is knowingly, in some cases, and unknowingly in others, systematically dismantling America as we know it today. Our debt is spiraling out of control at an unsustainable rate which, if not reined in soon, will put us on the level, financially, of many third world countries. Our military is slowly and methodically being dismantled, restrained, and reconstructed into an amoral institution. Our relations with formerly friendly countries, such as Israel, are at best, stressed, and little has been done to thwart our enemies, and reverse their pursuits on our nation! Moving the Israeli embassy to Jerusalem is a step in the right direction. Efforts were made on the part of our government, in the 2015 Israeli election, to defeat the American friendly, Bibi Netanyahu.

It is my strong belief that the feeble attempt by President Obama to slow ISIS, combined with the concerted effort to change Israel's power, was evidence of a deliberate plan to weaken America's status in the world posture, and to enable other powers to flourish.

Allowing a false mantra of "hands up don't shoot" to erode a once improving and healing racial divide, further evidenced a desire for "fundamental change of the United States of America!"

We are quickly becoming a welfare state dependent on the government, with intentions to do more of the same. There are calls to limit and even discontinue gun rights in the United States. The justice system was dramatically changing under Mr. Obama and would have soon limited or reduce the religious rights of Christian and conservative organizations that were opposed to the social and moral changes that were being made in our country. Lifetime appointments of liberal justice department lawyers and federal judges will eventually trump conservative decisions of states and local governments, if not reversed.

Not only was the military being intentionally redesigned, during the Obama administration, but police departments are being required to change (1997 Police Coordination Act, 1999 federal Police Investigation law) and would've eventually been militarized if proposed justice department efforts were enforced. The unrest in Ferguson, New York City, and Baltimore escalated the call for reform in local police departments. All of this, along with the recent executive branch of the government, demonstrating more control, during the Obama administration, pointed to "truth" being more and more distorted, changed, and manipulated.

We must seek and desire to know the truth. It is no longer reasonable to just trust our leadership, spiritual or civic, to do the right thing but "we the people," need to personally be hearing and trusting the word of God!

With the world changing as it is, and truth being accosted on every front, more people are searching for purpose and meaning in their life. Surprisingly, even born-again Christians are on the same search, when the answer is given to us in the book of John.

We think, just because we are Christians that all things should work out and make sense. God does have a plan for us, and He does want us to know His direction and purposes. He doesn't play hide-and-seek with us just for spite or sport. Rather, it is the Christian that hides from God. It is the Christian that distances himself until he finds a need for God. God is always in pursuit just to fellowship with us, and

He desires to have all that He can of our busy and distracted day.

I was raised (practically born) in a Southern Baptist Church. My family never missed church whether Sunday morning, Sunday night or Wednesday night. During revivals, the guest preacher had at least one meal and most of the time two meals in our home. We had, in our home, preachers like Bob Harrington, Angel Martinez, Major Ian Thomas, and W.A. Criswell to name a few.

I wasn't born saved but were it possible, it would have been true of me! I was never really challenged about my faith and what I believed until high school, and even then, those doing the challenging (usually classmates) were never able to form a defense for their beliefs either. It wasn't until college that my beliefs were really tested by unbelieving professors but again, I was defended by friends who knew more than I about what they really believed. Two of my college friends provided research for Josh McDowell's book, *Evidence That Demands a Verdict*, one of the best books written on apologetics. These were the friends who delivered my defense when debating our professors. So, again I didn't really need to know what I believed even during my college days.

I was a nine-year-old boy when I prayed to receive Christ and a senior in high school when I knew God wanted me in the ministry of some kind. But it was after I was married, and my kids were almost grown that I really discovered what I call "The Truth Principle."

My wife and I were beginning to see the last of our four children get married and begin a life of their own. We were in the stage of being settled, and life slowing down just a little (right before grandkids!)

Much of the Christian world is quickly reaching or has already become retirement age. Sadly, many interpret retirement to mean that we must retire spiritually as well, when in fact, the retired are better equipped, financially more stable, and physically have more time and freedom to give than ever before. The greatest resources, retired Christians, are *leaving* the battle! The least we could do, as "retired Christians," is to train, teach, finance, and send the younger folks into the battle, supplied, and prepared for it. We are the Generals. We need to lead!

Each of us, no matter our age, can be used by God to fulfill His purpose. Don't believe the lie that you are too young or too old, or that you are not gifted enough to accomplish something for God. The truth is "we can do all things through Christ!" We have won the battle.

A preacher once said, "I have read the back of the book, and we win!" Our goal is not to "win," but to proclaim the truth, and to bring as many as we can with us into the kingdom. He was correct that the Bible tells us that one day Satan will be defeated, and God's final kingdom will be set up.

Until that day, our work is not completed. Stay in the battle and keep the faith. Know, believe, speak, and live the truth!

"For the wrath of God is revealed from heaven against all ungodliness and unrighteousness of <u>men who suppress the truth</u> in unrighteousness, because that which is known about God is evident within them; for God made it evident to them. For since the creation of the world His invisible attributes, His eternal power, and divine nature, have been clearly seen, being understood through what has been made, so that they are <u>without excuse</u>." (Romans 1:18-20)

God, through nature, and His incredible creativity, through His massive and indescribable works, and through His unattainable and unfathomable design, has clearly shown Himself to the world. Rather than accept what God has undoubtedly and plainly revealed, man with his finite mind seeks other possible answers as an escape and seemingly guiltless answer to their sin.

"See to it that no one takes you captive through philosophy and empty deception, according to the tradition of men, according to the elementary principles of the world, rather than according to Christ." (Colossians 2:8)

He is the **way**, and the **truth**, and the **life**; no one comes to the Father but through Him! And that's the TRUTH!

Chapter 16: The Truth in Media

The Appellate Court of Florida's Second District in February 2003, unanimously agreed with an assertion by FOX News, that there is no rule against distorting or falsifying the news in the United States, as decided in the Akre-Wilson case against Fox.

Because of the FCC's loose regulations in respect to misrepresenting the truth, media organizations including television, radio, and print media have taken unprecedented freedom in reporting their version of "truth!"

In my Mass Communications major in college, it was stressed that students be sure of their sources and that the facts of their reporting be accurate and true. I remember one professor saying emphatically, "If there is any doubt at all about the facts, do not report it!" We were strongly encouraged as reporters to leave personal opinions out of our reporting, period! The only avenue available for a personal opinion was that of an editorial.

The "editorial," and the ethics and integrity associated with its purpose have all but disappeared from American media. Lies, intending to deceive the American public for political reasons, have become common and expected behavior of both liberal and conservative campaigns. The media, however, have become an obvious and deliberate advantage to the liberal agenda by propagating their socialist agenda.

The Federal Communications Commission has been derelict in its duty to discuss the need for guidelines and serious enforcement of media integrity. No one is suggesting guidelines which would infringe on the First Amendment, but deliberate falsehoods on the part of the media should have serious and explicit consequences.

Congress should be investigating laws that would hold the media accountable for truth in reporting, and the deliberate lying at the expense of public truthfulness.

Political pundits in all parties should unequivocally pursue a moral and ethical path in the interest of America's integrity. If the parties truly have the best interest of America in mind, there should be no disagreement of the necessity for change.

My optimism for the political parties to be willing to change their destructive tactics of terminating their opponents at any cost, even lying, is very slim. The expectation that the media will ever change and return to a fairly ethical position is even smaller.

As I explained in the last chapter, a deliberate and intentional dismantling of America, and more specifically Christianity, is in progress. Some of the offenders may be unaware of the spiritual battle, and even the scope of the political battle, but the lure of power outweighs their deception.

The dishonesty in our world, the decline of truth politically, the strategy of the Secular Humanist's, and the consequence of a dishonest media, have completely been fooled by the enemy of all times, Satan! "The thief comes to "steal, kill and destroy!" (John 10:10a)

The Church, for the most part, has been silent and ineffective, but not for long. One day, "every knee will bow...and every tongue will confess that Jesus Christ is Lord!" (Philippians 2:10-11)

On that day, when Christ returns, the politicians, the humanists, the media, and everyone who denied Christ as Savior and Lord will be exposed in front of all creation. Their power, wealth, and position will all be laid at the feet of Jesus.

My prayer is that many will repent of their ways and see the truth of their deceit before it is too late. The Christian hopes that the days when God pours out His Spirit upon the earth are near, and revival will sweep the land. My personal interpretation of scripture is that the "Church" will be raptured out before the tribulation.

Regardless of the timeline of Christ's return, today is the day of salvation and as many as receive Him as Savior and Lord will have eternal life!

TRUTH

Summary of the Truth Principle

This summary is included to give you a helpful outline of the *Truth Principle*, which will enable you to encourage others who may someday need your support when seeking answers.

It is important to emphasize that truth does exist in every aspect of our lives and that we need to examine what that truth actually is, and then apply it to our circumstances.

First, *Truth with God* is very important when beginning the truth process. God already knows everything about us, but He wants us to openly admit our disobedience and restore our fellowship with him. God is approachable and will respond to our honesty in love and acceptance.

Second, and most importantly, the *Truth of God's Word* is the standard by which we judge our lives, and what we believe about ourselves. Satan wants us to believe the lies of which he is convincing us, but when we know the truth; the truth will set us free! Approach each lie, fear, anger, lust gossip, or whatever it may be with the truth of God's word. It is important to read, memorize, and know the truth of God's Word. Remember, "Take every thought captive to the obedience of Christ," and don't allow that thought to move from your mind to your will, and become an emotional stronghold! The Bible is the standard for truth! Ask yourself, "What is the truth about this?" Believe the truth, not the lie!

Next, we discussed *Truth in Relationships* and the importance of healing and maintaining your relationships with others, past and present. The first two steps are sometimes easier than maintaining your relationships because this step requires, in most cases, going to a person and discussing your faults. It is important to determine honestly whether you are the problem or the solution. In completing this step, the true intent of your heart is expressed.

Hearing the Truth is a step that takes discipline and dedication to your personal time alone with God! Just like any Godly earthly father, our Heavenly Father also wants to have a deep personal relationship with you. He has a burning desire for you to know, and hear His plan and purpose for you, and just how much He loves you! Take the time to not only make requests to God but to listen and hear His heart as well.

To *Believe the Truth* is to have confidence in the truth, and to know the plan and purpose God has for you, then, employ His plan in the world and communities around you. Believing is to put your trust in, adhere to, and stick like glue to the truth of God's word.

When you have confidence in the truth, to *Live the Truth* is a natural result of the moral integrity and character that you gain from the author of truth. People will see, in you, the character of God, and the principles you have as you live out the truth around them. "Be fed, feed yourself, and feed others!"

Speak the Truth, in love, and be bold as a voice for truth when others may choose to be silent. Many people are living with the influence of lies in their lives and are screaming deep inside to know the truth. Be ready to offer the truth, when appropriate, to those who open the door to you. Sometimes, speaking the truth may be needed even when it's not comfortable to do so. Speak truth against strongholds, speak the truth to others, and speak the truth in confrontation when appropriate.

Move your prayer life from simple mundane recitations to the powerful application of God's word. We are promised that His Word "will not return void!" *Pray the Truth* when you pray. God's Word is power, authority, and truth; apply that power, authority, and truth to your praying.

Proclaim the Truth! Truth is not to be hidden but is to be proclaimed to the world! While many proclaim messages to the world which contain little or no truth and may, in fact, be destructive to the truth, it's important for those of us with truth to be proclaimers of the truth. Proclaim means to broadcast. Proclaiming is not simply speaking the truth when appropriate, but unapologetically broadcasting it!

Finally, *Desire the Truth.* We find ourselves with many projects pulling at us from every direction and robbing us of the time it may take to really focus on a desire for truth. Be one who's not only fed but one who is feeding others! It's not easy, but it is important to allow God to instill in us, a real and passionate desire to follow and pursue truth.

Don't allow yourself to retreat into the trap of lies which manipulate you back to a depressed and purposeless life. Ask God to instill within you the desire to know, hear, believe, live, speak, pray, proclaim, and desire the truth. Believe the TRUTH, not the lie!

Jesus said of Himself, "I am the way, and the truth, and the life; no one comes to the Father but through me." If one believes Jesus to be God as He claims, and it isn't true, nothing is lost. If one believes Jesus NOT to be God, and it IS true, that person has lost EVERYTHING!

ABOUT THE AUTHOR

Andy Dietz is the author of *Kidnapped in Budapest,* a story of his abduction and escape. He is a contributing author of *The Chosen Path,* a 360-day devotional book including contributions from Billy Graham, Zig Ziegler, and many others.

Aside from writing, Andy spent thirteen years traveling with his twin brother Phil, singing across America, and on a USO tour to the Caribbean Islands. Andy later spent thirty-three years in student ministry and missions to three churches with as many as seven hundred students attending.

One of Andy's passions has been missions, with his travel to over forty countries including a nineteen-year medical effort in China, a ten-year commitment to an orphanage in Mexico, and five years of evangelism in Budapest, Hungary.

In recent years, Andy and his wife Becky have facilitated four to six Pastor/wife retreats a year with Double Honor Ministries of Oklahoma and are leading *Finding Your Purpose* conferences with churches on weekends.

Andy also pastors a church in West Texas and still finds time to spend with his four married children and eleven grandchildren.

In his spare time, Andy has discovered his ability to paint and draw. Josiah, one of his six grandsons, recently ask Andy to draw a picture of him. To everyone's amazement, the drawing looked just like Josiah (top left). Needless to say, all the grandkids wanted a drawing!

Andy's greatest passion, aside from his family, is that of his passion for people around the world to know the truth!

Kidnapped In Budapest

The chilling true story of Andy's kidnapping.

By Andy Dietz

In the book, Andy recounts the traumatic events that would change his life and his view of God forever!

Available on amazon.com

The Story of My Life

An Unbelievable Journey

By Andy Dietz

True stories of travel, tragedy, music, and celebrities. Stories of my life that will make you laugh, will make you cry, and will even surprise you.

Stories about; Bob Hope, Johnny Carson, Ray Stevens, Steve Martin, Roger Miller, Jerry Clower, Karen Carpenter, The Nitty Gritty Dirt Band, Tennessee Ernie Ford, and many others. Stories that will inspire you to change the world!

Available on amazon.com

ME? Change The World?

Finding Your Purpose

By Andy Dietz

Many people choose to just exist, rather than living out their God given purpose!

Their job, or school, or family become their life, rather than finding their calling! This book helps the reader find that one passion that is given by God.

Available on Amazon.com

Fear Is A Liar

Believing the truth, not the lie!

By Andy Dietz

Battling fear, anger, depression, insecurity or any other stronghold in your life? *Fear Is A Liar* reveals answers for overcoming these and other struggles with TRUTH and living a life of purpose.

Available on amazon.com

First-Aid Kit For Pastors

Calling Never Accepts Quitting

By Andy Dietz

This book is a tool for new and seasoned pastors with help and ideas to bring unity and purpose to your staff and congregations. Also included, are Tools to strengthen your family and relationship with your spouse.

Available on amazon.com

FIRST-AID KIT
For Pastors

Calling Never Accepts
Quitting!

ANDY DIETZ

Time Alone With God

104 Weekly Devotionals

By Andy Dietz

This is A two year collection of devotionals drawn form my person daily quite times. These devotionals were inspired by some of my favorite passages in the Bible, and prompted memories of stories from the past.

Available on amazon.com

Time Alone With God

TAWG
Weekly Devotionals
ANDY DIETZ

Made in the USA
Coppell, TX
23 December 2023

26842574R00108